WALKING
BY THE SPIRIT

BIBLE
MODULAR
SERIES

Bob Jones University Press, Greenville, South Carolina 29614

This textbook was written by members of the faculty and staff of Bob Jones University. Standing for the "old-time-religion" and the absolute authority of the Bible since 1927, Bob Jones University is the world's leading Fundamentalist Christian university. The staff of the University is devoted to educating Christian men and women to be servants of Jesus Christ in all walks of life.

Providing unparalleled academic excellence, Bob Jones University prepares its students through its offering of over one hundred majors, while its fervent spiritual emphasis prepares their minds and hearts for service and devotion to the Lord Jesus Christ.

If you would like more information about the spiritual and academic opportunities available at Bob Jones University, please call
1-800-BJ-AND-ME (1-800-252-6363).
www.bju.edu

NOTE:

The fact that materials produced by other publishers may be referred to in this volume does not constitute an endorsement by Bob Jones University Press of the content or theological position of materials produced by such publishers. The position of Bob Jones University Press, and of the University itself, is well known. Any references and ancillary materials are listed as an aid to the student or the teacher and in an attempt to maintain the accepted academic standards of the publishing industry.

Walking by the Spirit

Damon Amato, M.A.

Project Editor: Manda Kalagayan
Design: John Bjerk
Composition: Jennifer Hearing

CONTENTS

*I*ntroduction:
Why Study the Holy Spirit?. v

*G*aining New Knowledge 1

*G*aining New Life 17

*G*od's Temple. 31

*C*hrist's Body 45

*E*quipped to Serve 61

*E*nabled to Walk. 85

*P*romised Glory 103

*C*onclusion:
How Then Shall We Walk? 119

Why Study the Holy Spirit?

Speaking from his pulpit at St. Mark's in Van Nuys, California, in 1960, Dennis Bennett declared to his congregation that he had experienced the Holy Spirit in a new way, a way that had allowed him to speak in unknown, ecstatic tongues. Bennett recounted to his audience that he had met with a couple and prayed together with them. During his prayer, he received the power to speak "other words" that he was unable to understand himself. But he was sure that something powerful had happened and that he had experienced the deeper encounter that he had been longing for. Though his announcement was not received well by his Episcopal congregation, it marked the beginning of the Charismatic movement and a renewed interest in the gifts of the Holy Spirit and His operations today.

In Toronto, Rev. Rodney Howard-Browne encourages and promotes holy laughter in the name of the Holy Spirit. According to Pastor David Brown, Howard-Browne "tells a lot of jokes and rattles off one-liners before encouraging people to let the spirit flow 'out of the belly' in holy laughter." The *Christian Research Journal* reported that "some laugh hysterically. Some topple over or crumble silently on the floor, while others jerk, twitch, keel drunkenly, . . . scream, sway, . . . roar, or bark." The laughing experience lasts about an hour and supposedly represents the joy of

PhotoDisc, Inc.

the Holy Ghost. Howard-Browne usually begins the frenzy himself by slowly increasing his laughing. Many who have been "smitten" with laughter claim that it is a visible manifestation of the Holy Spirit's work. In an interview with Julia Dulin, Howard-Browne explained how his holy laughter began with a prayer in 1979. He prayed, "'Either You come down here and touch me, or I will come up there and touch You.' . . . Suddenly, his whole body felt like it was on fire. He began to laugh uncontrollably. Then he wept and began to speak in tongues. 'I was plugged into heaven's electrical supply,' he later wrote in his book, *The Touch of God.* 'And since then my desire has been to go and plug other people in.'" Since that time, hundreds of thousands of people have flocked to his church, Toronto Airport Vineyard, and thousands claim to have been smitten with the holy laughter.

Are these manifestations true? Are they really from the Holy Spirit? Unfortunately, many Christians do not have enough solid teaching concerning the Spirit to evaluate these events. Although they may sense that these so-called manifestations of the Spirit are false, many could not answer crucial questions concerning the Spirit, particularly concerning His work in the life of the believer. What about you? How would you answer the following questions?

Does Scripture support the deity of the Holy Spirit? If so, how?

What specific activities does the Holy Spirit perform in the salvation of a sinner?

What is the believer's relationship to the Holy Spirit?

How should a Christian evaluate modern claims regarding tongues and Spirit baptism?

Much of this material may be unfamiliar territory. However, all of it is important if you are to understand current movements and trends. There is another, more personal reason for studying what the Bible reveals about the Holy Spirit. Learning about the person and work of the Holy Spirit is vitally important for your walk with Christ. Do you realize that you cannot serve Christ apart from walking in the Spirit? Do you realize that you cannot know God's will without the Spirit's instruction? Your relationship to the Spirit is vital for your Christian walk with God and for your success in overcoming sin. So vital, in fact, that Christ said it was better that He went away in order that the Comforter would come (John 16:7). That's amazing! Christ is saying that believers are in a better position with the Spirit's ministry than if Christ had continued His earthly ministry. Since that's true, we definitely need to know more about the Spirit.

The importance of studying the Spirit, though, goes beyond just refuting error and understanding His ministry. We must live in submission to the Spirit if we are to render proper service to the Lord. Just as our thinking must change concerning the Spirit, so also our attitude and will must change.

Practically Perfect

Let me ask you a question. Have you ever known a person who thought he was spiritual because of the amount of service he did for the church? He sang in the choir, gave his tithes regularly, and showed up to mow the lawn when it was his turn. He even stayed late to help clean up after the church fellowships. He had confused service for spirituality. No amount of activity and service, however, can make a person "spiritual." Real spirituality is measured by your relationship with and submission to the Spirit.

Finally, understanding the work of the Spirit and applying what you learn about Him will be life-changing. By the end of this study, you should be able to evaluate movements that claim the power of the Spirit. But more importantly, you should have a closer walk with Christ. It is my prayer that this book will help you to have a Spirit-filled walk and that "the God of our Lord Jesus Christ, the Father of glory, may give unto you the spirit of wisdom and revelation in the knowledge of him: the eyes of your understanding being enlightened" (Eph. 1:17-18).

CHAPTER ONE

Gaining New Knowledge

Getting to know someone takes more than just casual thought or an occasional meeting. When I first met my wife, it was at her campus apartment. I had stopped by to talk to one of her roommates who was from Jerusalem. (I had written a short story in Modern Hebrew and was hoping for a brief evaluation of its grammatical correctness. I am sure that it was this nerd-like quality that first caught my wife's eye.) Anyway, she answered the door, and we chatted for a moment. After that, we began a wonderful relationship. But it wasn't for a few months that I really began to know her. I began to understand her by what she said or didn't say, how she acted or reacted to different circumstances, and what she approved of and disapproved of. To summarize, I had to take the time and effort to really know who she was. And it has paid rich rewards.

Similarly, if we are going to know who the Spirit is, we must pay attention to what He has said about Himself in His Word. We must notice His actions and attributes. Careful consideration of His titles will help us to understand how He relates to us and to God the Father and God the Son. In short, we must begin to know who the Spirit really is.

The Holy Spirit Is a Person

His Personality

The Holy Spirit possesses personality. He is not just power; that erroneous notion is far too common today. As a person, the Holy Spirit has a will, an intellect, and emotions. Those three traits exclude all impersonal objects. The earth may rotate on its axis, but it doesn't choose to do so (nor does it feel happy when it does). A rock does not make a conscious decision to be eroded by water, and wind doesn't get offended when a mountain blocks its blowing. Only a person can choose, think, and feel. And because the Holy Spirit displays all three qualities, we unquestionably know that He is a person.

Let me give you some examples. First Corinthians 12:11 teaches that the Holy Spirit chooses to give gifts. They are under His control and will. In Acts 16:6-7, the Spirit made the decision that Paul would not go into certain regions to preach the Word. Both of these passages teach that He has a will. Concerning His intellect, I Corinthians 2:10-11 states, "But God hath revealed them unto us by his Spirit: for the Spirit searcheth all things, yea, the deep things of God. For what man knoweth the things of a man, save the spirit of man which is in him? even so the things of God knoweth no man, but the Spirit of God." This passage teaches that the Spirit alone can search the depth of the knowledge of God. In order to do so, the Spirit must have an unlimited intellect. Finally, the Bible explains that the Spirit has emotions. John 14-16 tells us that He loves us just as Christ does, and Romans 15:30 calls Him the Spirit of love. Just as we can displease the Father who loves us, we can also displease the

Only a person can choose, think, and feel.

2

Spirit. According to Ephesians 4:30, we can grieve the Spirit by not obeying. That truth is a sobering reality. Our prayer should be that God would keep us from causing the Holy Spirit to be saddened by our unsubmissiveness to Him.

One final note can be added concerning the personality of the Spirit. In addition to recording the Spirit's will, intellect, and emotion, the Bible records that the Spirit talked to the disciples. In Acts 8:29, the Spirit spoke to Philip and directed him to the eunuch: "Then the Spirit said unto Philip, Go near, and join thyself to this chariot." In Acts 10:19-20, the Spirit spoke to Peter and informed him about the coming three visitors from Cornelius:

"While Peter thought on the vision, the Spirit said unto him, Behold, three men seek thee. Arise therefore, and get thee down, and go with them, doubting nothing: for I have sent them." And in Acts 13, the Holy Spirit spoke to the church and instructed the people to separate Paul and Barnabas for the first missionary journey. He then sent them out of the church. All of these examples prove that the Spirit is a person.

His Names

Within the Bible, names and titles reveal the character or nature of a person. This is especially true of God. God often reveals truths about Himself through names. For instance, God could have said that He would care for all of our needs, including food and clothing, because of our filial relationship to Him. Instead, He calls Himself our Father. God could have said that Christ would be the powerful ruler who would effect tranquility on the earth. Instead, He called Him the Prince of Peace. Likewise, the Bible could have referred to the Spirit as just "the Spirit" throughout the Bible, but often it states that He is the Holy Spirit. In fact, that designation is the most common name given to the third person of the Trinity. The title appears ninety-three times within the Bible, ninety of those times within the New Testament. The Spirit was obviously pointing out that the central characteristic of His being is holiness. The Spirit is infinitely holy and pure; that is the reason that He cannot indwell sinners. The Spirit must dwell in someone that has been cleansed and purified, someone that can be likened to the temple, where He descended in glory.

Another common name for the third person of the Trinity is the Spirit of God or Spirit of the Lord. This title accentuates His deity. You could take this title to mean "the Spirit who is God." The Spirit is also called the Spirit of truth three times in John 14-16 (14:17; 15:26; 16:13) and once in I John 5:6. This title calls our attention to the fact that the Spirit imparts truth to the believer. He is the one who leads the believer to what is true and faithful. You can follow the Spirit's leading because He is a Spirit of truth. In Zechariah 12:10, He is called the Spirit of grace and supplication. I love that title. It points to the beautiful work of the Spirit whereby He does a work of grace in our souls to make us sorrowful for our sins, so that we turn in supplication to the Lord.

In John 14-16, the Spirit is called the Comforter four times (14:16, 26; 15:26; 16:7). This title highlighted the Spirit's future ministry to the disciples as One who would continue to intercede,

What is blasphemy of the Spirit? Can a person commit it today?

In Matthew 12:31-32, Mark 3:29, and Luke 12:10, Jesus states that whoever blasphemes the Holy Spirit will never be forgiven. Let's start with the context. In Matthew 12:22, Christ healed a demon-possessed man who was blind and mute. This miracle was an amazing demonstration of the Spirit's power on Christ's life. All the crowds were amazed at the miracle and were wondering if Jesus was the Messiah. The Pharisees heard the crowds' words and responded that Jesus cast out demons only by the power of Beelzebub, the ruler of the demons. The Pharisees willingly rejected the testimony of the Spirit to Jesus' Messiahship. Instead, they said that Jesus was working miracles by Satan, thereby attacking the Spirit's holiness and rejecting His testimony. This sin demonstrated a complete hardness of heart by the Pharisees; it also marked the end of the Spirit's striving with them. He would no longer convict them of their sin. It was an unforgivable sin.

Now, can a person commit this sin today? If the same circumstances were reproduced, a person could technically blaspheme the Spirit. However, the circumstances would require Christ's earthly ministry again. Therefore, it is not possible to blaspheme the Spirit in the same way today. However, Scripture does teach that God may stop convicting a person from sin if he does not repent (Gen. 6:3). The person may not have committed blasphemy of the Spirit, but he has resisted God. That should compel you, if you are unsaved and fighting God's Spirit, to repent immediately. God will not always strive with you.

teach, and abide with them. Jesus was sending a Paraclete (that's the Greek word behind the English word *Comforter*) that would minister to them in a manner similar to that of His own earthly ministry. The Spirit would guide and lead them inwardly as Christ had led them outwardly. In Acts 9:31, we see a direct fulfillment of this as the church everywhere continued in the "comfort of the Holy Ghost."

Other titles for the Spirit that appear within the Bible include the Spirit of glory (I Pet. 4:14), the Spirit of adoption (Rom. 8:15), and the Spirit of life (Rom. 8:2). Again, all of these titles of the Spirit highlight some aspect of His person or ministry to the believer.

Read the words of the following hymn by Simon Browne. What titles does Browne call attention to explicitly as well as implicitly?

Come, Gracious Spirit, Heavenly Dove

Come, gracious Spirit, heav'nly Dove.
With light and comfort from above;
Be Thou our Guardian, Thou our Guide;
O'er every tho't and step preside.

The light of truth to us display,
And make us know and choose Thy way;
Plant holy fear in every heart,
That we from God may ne'er depart.

Lead us to holiness, the road
Which we must take to dwell with God;
Lead us to Christ, the living Way,
Nor let us from His presence stray.

Lead us to God, our final rest,
To be with Him forever blest
Lead us to heav'n, that we may share
Fullness of joy forever there.

The Holy Spirit Is God

He Is Identified as God

The Holy Spirit is identified as deity in several ways throughout the Bible. In Acts 5, a married couple who really wanted the attention and congratulations of the church and apostles brought an offering to the Lord. Supposedly, the offering represented all of the money that they had received from selling a portion of land. They laid the money at the apostles' feet and stood waiting for "praise the Lord, brother" and pats on the back. But instead of receiving the praise of men, Ananias and Sapphira received heart-piercing words from Peter. Peter stated, "Why hath Satan filled thine heart to lie to the Holy Ghost, and to keep back part of the price of the land? . . . Thou hast not lied unto men, but unto God" (Acts 5:3-4). Notice the careful selection of Peter's words. He first states that the couple lied to the Holy Spirit, and then He states that the couple lied to God. He is equating the two as the same person. In other words, he is affirming that the couple lied to God the Spirit. Though Peter was directly dealing with their hypocrisy and pretense of being Spirit-led, he was indirectly affirming the deity of the Spirit. He was also demonstrating that the Spirit wasn't just a thing or a power. He is a person who can be lied to; He is God, and He struck the couple dead for their hypocrisy.

The Spirit's deity can also be demonstrated by His inclusion within the Trinitarian formulas in the New Testament. By Trinitarian formula we mean verses that include or mention all three persons of the Godhead in one statement or narrative. These statements show that

The Bible is placing all three persons of the Godhead on an equal level.

the Spirit is coequal with the Father and the Son. For example, Matthew 28:19 states, "Go ye therefore, and teach all nations, baptizing them in the name of the Father, and of the Son, and of the Holy Ghost." Another example of a Trinitarian passage is Matthew 3:16-17: "And Jesus, when he was baptized, went up straightway out of the water: and, lo, the heavens were opened unto him, and he saw the Spirit of God descending like a dove, and lighting upon Him: And lo a voice from heaven, saying, This

Going in Deeper!

Corel Corporation

Think About It!

Have you ever wondered how the Bible can present each member of the Godhead as coequal, and yet the Son as subordinate to the Father and the Spirit as subordinate to the Son? Good question. Although each person of the Trinity is coequal, or coessential (that's the theological term that means equal in essence or being), the Son subordinates Himself to the Father, and the Spirit subordinates Himself to the Son. This subordination is called economic subordination. It has nothing to do with the status of the person but rather with his function or job. If you still don't understand how this works, don't worry; it's a mystery that we must accept by faith. However, it is a mystery that is not illogical, but supralogical—that is, it exceeds our reasoning capabilities. As Paul writes in Romans 11:33 after exploring a different mystery, "O the depth of the riches both of the wisdom and knowledge of God!"

is my beloved Son, in whom I am well pleased." Notice that all three persons—God the Father, God the Son, and God the Spirit—are mentioned in this passage. The Bible is placing all three persons of the Godhead on an equal level. It is suggesting that the Holy Spirit is God.

Finally, because He is God, the Holy Spirit even takes the name of Jehovah in the Old Testament. Jehovah is the name of God that represents His absolute freedom and independence from all creation. He is not bound by any limits. It also is His special covenant name used by His chosen people. For someone to ascribe this name to someone who is not God is absolute blasphemy. So when the Bible ascribes this name to the Spirit, it is clearly teaching that the Spirit is deity. A good example is Paul's use of Isaiah 6:9-10, which states that Jehovah said to Isaiah, "Go, and tell this people, Hear ye indeed, but understand not; and see ye indeed, but perceive not." But in Acts 28:25-26, Paul attributes these words to the Holy Spirit: "Well spake the Holy Ghost by Esaias the prophet unto our fathers, Saying, Go unto this people, and say, Hearing ye shall hear, and shall not understand." Paul certainly believed that the Holy Spirit was God and could be assigned the name of Jehovah. A similar reference occurs in Hebrews 3:7-11, which quotes Psalm 95:7-11.

He Possesses Divine Attributes

Divine attributes are ascribed to the Holy Spirit throughout the Bible. These attributes, or personal characteristics, are true only of God. To use an analogy from chemistry, if an element has 79 protons, an atomic mass of 197.0, and an electron configuration of 2, 8, 18, 32, 18, 1, then it must be gold. The element cannot be anything else. Likewise, if the Spirit pos-

sesses the qualities of deity, He must be God. What are some of these quali- ties or attributes of deity? Well, first, He is omniscient—He knows everything: "Who hath directed the Spirit of the Lord, or being his counsellor hath taught him?" (Isa. 40:13). The Spirit of God has no need for someone to instruct Him. He has known all things since eternity past. As mentioned before, I Corinthians 2:10-11 states that the Spirit alone can search the omniscience of God, because the Spirit is omniscient.

If the Spirit possesses the qualities of deity, He must be God.

He is also omnipresent, which means that He is everywhere: "Whither shall I go from thy spirit? or whither shall I flee from thy presence?" (Ps. 139:7). Because the Spirit is everywhere at all times, we can take great comfort as believers that we are never alone. Haggai had to remind Israel of this truth: "My spirit remaineth among you: fear ye not" (2:5). Next, the Holy Spirit is omnipotent as demonstrated by His work in Creation: "Thou sendest forth thy spirit, they are created" (Ps. 104:30). Genesis 1 also states that it was the Spirit who sat brooding on the face of the water. Only an omnipotent being could bring life out of nothing. The Spirit is also eternal: "How much more shall the blood of Christ, who through the eter- nal Spirit offered himself without spot to God, purge your conscience from dead works to serve the living God" (Heb. 9:14). The characteristic of eternality belongs solely to God. No being can duplicate it, and it is not possessed by humans. The Holy Spirit is also attributed the characteristic of wisdom, a characteristic that He bestows on people employed in the service of God (Exod. 28:3; 31:3; 35:31; Deut. 34:9; Isa. 11:2).

In the book of Revelation, the Spirit is attributed perfection in a peculiar way: He is called the seven Spirits of God (1:4; 3:1; 4:5; 5:6). At first this designation may seem to indicate a multiplicity of Spirits, but we must interpret carefully, beginning with the fact that Revelation 1:4-5 is a Trinitarian passage. John greets the churches with grace from God the Father (He that is, and who was, and who will be), God the Spirit (the seven Spirits), and God the Son (Jesus). Because He has carefully integrated this title within a Trinitarian statement, we may correctly identify the seven Spirits as the Holy Spirit. Next, we also know that the number seven sometimes designates perfection or completion in the Bible. If we plug that knowledge into these passages, we realize that the Holy Spirit is the perfect Spirit, the perfect God. Lastly, Revelation 3 begins by stating that the message to the church of Sardis is from the seven Spirits, but verse 6 concludes by stating that the message is from the Spirit. Taking all of these verses into consideration, we conclude that the phrase "seven Spirits" refers to the perfect Holy Spirit of God.

He Accomplishes Divine Works

The Holy Spirit also performs divine works. Some of His works are in the physical realm, such as miracles (I Kings 18:12; II Kings 2:16; Heb. 2:4) and Creation (Gen. 1:2), whereas other works are spiritual, such as the regeneration of a sinner. "Jesus answered, Verily, verily, I say unto thee, Except a man be born of water and of the Spirit, he cannot enter into the kingdom of God" (John 3:5). The Holy Spirit also indwells the believer: "He that raised up Christ from the dead shall also quicken your mortal bodies by his Spirit that dwelleth in you" (Rom. 8:11). Although the miracle of the virgin birth can never be fully understood, we know that it was the Holy Spirit who came upon Mary and brought about the conception of Jesus: "The Holy Ghost shall come upon thee, and the power of the Highest shall overshadow thee" (Luke 1:35); "for that which is conceived in her is of the Holy Ghost" (Matt. 1:20; see also verse 18). The Holy Ghost also baptizes, anoints, seals, and gifts believers. All of these works overwhelmingly point to His deity. He is God.

Another work of the Spirit that Scripture teaches is the work of inspiration and revelation. The Old Testament states in various ways that the authors of Scripture always wrote what was revealed to them by the Spirit. In Numbers 11 Moses prophesied by the Spirit, as did the elders when they were empowered by the Spirit (11:17, 25, 26, 29). In II Samuel 23:2, David directly claims that he spoke by the Spirit; Christ verifies that claim in Mark 12:36 and in Matthew 22:43. David also received the pattern of the temple by the Spirit (I Chron. 28:12). In II Chronicles the Spirit empowered Azariah (15:1), Jahaziel (20:14), and Zechariah (24:20) to prophesy and reveal God's Word to the people. We find in Nehemiah that the Levites called the Spirit "thy good spirit" whom God sent to instruct them (9:20) and that the Lord had admonished the people through the prophets by His Spirit (9:30). Ezekiel claims eleven times that the Spirit of the Lord was inspiring the revelations that he saw and recorded (2:2; 3:12, 14, 24; 8:3; 11:1, 5, 24; 37:1; 43:5). The last Old Testament reference to the Spirit's inspiring prophets is in Zechariah 7:12: "Yea, they made their hearts as an adamant stone, lest they should hear the law, and the words which the Lord of hosts hath sent in his Spirit by the former prophets."

In the New Testament, we find some of the same claims of inspiration and revelation by the Spirit. In the book of Luke, Zacharias, the father of John the Baptist, prophesied by the Holy Spirit (1:67); Simeon, a priest on whom was the Spirit, received revelation concerning the Messiah by the Spirit and was also led by the Spirit to the temple to see Jesus (2:25-27). In Acts, Agabus prophesied by the Spirit twice: once about a coming great famine (11:28) and once about Paul's approaching afflictions (21:11). The Holy Spirit also testified directly to Paul about his coming affliction (20:23). In Ephesians, Paul claims that it is the Holy Spirit that revealed to him the mystery about Christ. According to the book of Hebrews, it was the Holy Spirit who was signifying by the ceremonial laws in the Old Testament that Christ was not come yet (9:8). Hebrews also claims that it was the Holy Spirit bearing us witness in Jeremiah 31 (10:15). And in the book of Revelation, John claims to be "in the Spirit" before each section of the book (1:10; 4:2; 17:3; 21:10). John also stresses the necessity of hearing what the Spirit says to the seven churches (2:7, 11, 17, 29; 3:6, 13, 22).

Lastly, we have a direct statement of inspiration by the Spirit in the New Testament. Second Peter 1:21 teaches that all the writers of the Old Testament wrote as they were moved by the Holy Spirit. The verb *moved* in this verse designates something that is carried along by another thing or person, like a ship by the wind. In fact, that is exactly how the verb is used in Acts 27:15. The men could not fight the wind, so they let the wind carry the ship. God the Spirit guaranteed that what the Old Testament and New Testament writers wrote was absolutely the Word of God. He inspired them and ensured that every word was the Word from the mouth of God.

All of these references conclusively demonstrate that the writers of the Bible were aware that they were inspired by the Spirit to write Holy Scripture. They knew His presence and influence as they wrote. The Holy Spirit is unquestionably the source and author of the Holy Scriptures.

Summary

The following list summarizes the concepts addressed in this chapter. Many of the verses listed explicitly point to the deity of the Spirit. Read the verses and ponder their significance to your understanding of the Holy Spirit and His work.

1. The Spirit has a will (Acts 16:6-7; I Cor. 12:11).
2. He has an intellect (I Cor. 2:10-11).
3. He has emotion (Eph. 4:30).
4. He is called God (Acts 5:3-4).
5. He is called Jehovah (Isa. 6:9-10 and Acts 28:25-27; Ps. 95:7-11 and Heb. 3:7-11).
6. He is eternal (Heb. 9:14).
7. He is omnipotent (Ps. 104:30; Rom. 15:19).
8. He is omniscient (I Cor. 2:10-11; Isa. 40:13-14).
9. He is omnipresent (Ps. 139:7-10).
10. He creates (Gen. 1:2; Job 26:13; 33:4; Isa. 34:16).
11. He regenerates (John 3:5-6; Titus 3:5).
12. He inspired the Scriptures (Acts 1:16; 4:25; I Pet. 1:11).

Think About It

As I walked out of the souvenir shop of the airport hotel, I noticed several couches and armchairs scattered throughout the lobby. They were beckoning my weary legs to rest a moment before I went back to the terminal to catch my connecting flight (my flight had been delayed—an experience far too common for all of us). I strolled over to a red easy chair that was positioned by a lamp. Having set my backpack on the carpet, I yawned and stretched out my legs. I pulled my Bible out and began reading in the book of John. Within two minutes I was approached by a lady and her son and daughter. She was a Jehovah's Witness. As we talked, the subject of the Trinity came up, and she tried to explain to me her belief about the Spirit. She said, "The Spirit is not God. He is the divine force or mighty power of God. In other words," she clarified, "the Spirit is just a title for the manifestation of God's power. After all, God is one." Using the verse list above, could you defend that the Spirit is truly God? What key phrases in the verses support His deity?

Review Questions

1. Why are the names of God the Spirit important?

2. What is the most common name for God the Spirit? Why is this important?

3. How does Acts 5 identify the Holy Spirit as God?

4. What is a Trinitarian passage?

5. What are three divine attributes that the Spirit possesses? What passages in the Bible teach these attributes?

6. What passages teach that the Holy Spirit inspired Scripture?

7. The following paragraph is an excerpt from a theologian who does not believe in the Trinity. Evaluate his comments carefully; then, write a refutation using Scripture passages.

"The truth is obvious: To the Hebrews the Spirit of God was a force or essence that, though invisible, manifested itself in enhancing physical, intellectual or creative strength. . . . Conclusion? Something immaterial, impersonal but powerful and dynamic. . . . The Holy Spirit is neither the wild, uncontrollable force that takes over people and throws them into near hysteria nor is it the third person of the Trinity. God's Spirit is defined in the Bible as a power that can dwell in small measure inside a human mind and that inspires sound-mindedness and courage."—taken from *The Plain Truth* by Neil Earle

CHAPTER TWO

Gaining New Life

2

Conviction

Children are born wicked. I gave clear witness to this truth at an early age. My parents had instructed my siblings and me to wash up before bed and to brush our teeth. Being the youngest of the three at that time, I was lovingly pushed aside from the sink and persuaded to wait my turn. Though thoughts of defiance and standing my ground filled my mind, my three-inch biceps predicted to me what the obvious outcome would be. I chose to wait. When my siblings were finished, they left the bathroom a mess and me alone. I picked up my toothbrush and the new tube of toothpaste, remembering my parents' warning not to leave toothpaste on the sink.

But as I began to squeeze the toothpaste onto my brush, I became enthralled with the feeling of squirting this semiliquid substance. However, my toothbrush was not very long, so I decided to add some decoration to the bathroom. Making a grand circle around the sink, I looked about for other places to share my artistic flair. "What a plain toilet that is," I thought. So I squeezed a ring around the lid. I couldn't have made a more perfect circle had I made it with a compass. It was at this point, though, that I heard a deep, familiar voice calling my name. I was suddenly aware that I was no longer the only one in the bathroom. Turning around, I saw my father standing in the doorway. Although he had seen me squirting the toothpaste everywhere, he gave me a chance to speak. He questioned, "Did you squirt the toothpaste around the sink and toilet?" I elusively responded, "Did you see me?" My dad wasn't impressed. My standing with the tube in hand and the mess in sight was all the evidence that my father needed. The evidence declared me guilty, and I could not refute any of it. My forthcoming punishment was justly deserved. Though I had tried to avoid the guilt, I was convicted.

Conviction has nothing to do with the remorse of a person or lack thereof. It is totally objective in its nature. Legally, if a criminal is tried within a courtroom and the evidence proves him guilty, then he is convicted—despite whether he feels sorry for his crime. The evidence convinces the judge of his guiltiness. Likewise, the Bible states that all are guilty before God (Rom. 3:19). And it is the first work of grace by the Spirit that convinces a man about his need for the gospel.

What Is Conviction?

The conviction of the Holy Spirit is *the Holy Spirit's proving to the sinner that the gospel message is true.* Although the Spirit could use multiple methods to demonstrate the sinner's guiltiness, the Word of God is His ordained method—whether by sermon, lesson, or testimony. The Spirit takes God's Word and convicts the sinner of his sin. The sinner may then either repent of his sin or reject the conviction of the Holy Spirit, but he cannot refute the evidence that is brought forth.

The Spirit takes God's Word and convicts the sinner of his sin.

A person's being convicted of his sin does not necessarily mean that he will repent of it. In fact, some of the Old Testament Israelites rejected the conviction of the Spirit and refused to listen to His instruction. Stephen mentions this rejection in his address to the Jews in Acts 7:51. The book of Hebrews states that the rejection of the Holy Spirit's convicting grace is an insult to His person and invokes a severe punishment: "Of how much sorer punishment, suppose ye, shall he be thought worthy, who hath trodden under foot the Son of God, and hath counted the blood of the covenant, wherewith he was sanctified, an unholy thing, and hath done despite unto the Spirit of grace?" (10:29). According to this passage, the judgment for those who refused to listen to the Spirit's conviction will be severer than if they had never known this grace.

Whom and of What Does the Spirit Convict?

Having defined what conviction is, we need to know exactly whom the Spirit convicts and what the Spirit convicts him of. For answers to these questions, you need to look at John 16:8-11. In this passage, the word for convict is *reprove*. Now, notice whom He convicts—the world (v. 8). This term includes not only those who respond correctly to conviction and are saved but also those who reject the Spirit's conviction. Verses 9-11 explain what He will convict them of; they are the three points of the gospel message. First, the Holy Spirit convicts men about their sin, particularly their unbelief in Christ. In conviction, the Holy Spirit will show the person that he is a sinner, that he is desperately wicked.

Next, the Spirit convicts the person of righteousness. Although this may seem puzzling at first, Christ explains exactly what He means. The righteousness concerns Christ's going to the Father. During His earthly ministry, Christ claimed that after He died for the sins of the world, He would be resurrected and would go to the Father again. The Jews disbelieved this claim and asserted that Christ was blaspheming by claiming to be God. However, Acts tells us that Christ did indeed go to

Shot in the Neck, Convicted in the Heart

As you read the following story of James Gardiner's conversion, note the three areas of the Holy Spirit's conviction. Which aspect of conviction came last? Would Gardiner have been saved without this last area of conviction?

In 1706 James Gardiner fought in the Battle of Ramilles, another of Marlborough's daring and dangerous engagements aimed at driving the French back to their own borders. Deputed to clear the enemy out of an advantageous position they were occupying in a church-yard, Gardiner and his band of brave companions were succeeding to some extent when a shot from a French gun hit him in the mouth. Numbed, he fell to the ground, and wondered vaguely whether he had swallowed the missile when he discovered that his teeth and tongue were undamaged by the impact. As Gardiner tried to trace the course of the shot with his finger he realised that it had travelled through his mouth and out of his neck, only just missing his spinal cord.

Taught to fear God from earliest years, James knew that preservation of his life was little short of divine intervention on his behalf. For gun-shot to pass through his mouth and out from the back of his neck without killing him outright astonished the young soldier. And if God had spared his life in this way, he must also intend him to recover from his wound, reasoned Gardiner. . . . But no thought of humbling himself before his God as yet crossed the wounded soldier's mind.

God's time was approaching, however, when he would intervene in the life of this dissolute young man. One Sunday evening in July

1719, having completed his duties with his troops, Gardiner, now a major (for a further promotion had raised him to this rank), attended some function that did not finish until eleven o'clock at night. But Gardiner's evening was not over. . . . Having an hour to kill, he returned to his quarters, roaming restlessly around his room as the moments crawled by. With little better to do he picked up a small book that his anxious mother had concealed among his belongings. Being a military man, he found the title arresting: *The Christian Soldier, or Heaven Taken by Storm*, written by Thomas Watson, a well-known Puritan. Gardiner began to flip carelessly through its pages by the light of his candle. . . .

Scenes from the past flashed through Gardiner's mind: the earnest exhortations and prayers of his mother; the long night as he lay wounded on the battlefield; [and] . . . the many escapes from imminent danger. . . . [A]gainst the backdrop of such a catalogue of divine mercies, he saw his own ugly way of life: the heedless path of unbelief and those sordid sins which had polluted his mind and body to such an extent that he had once declared he could never relinquish them unless God provided him with a new body. Without doubt he was a candidate for the just retribution of God's anger and for final damnation. Why God had not already struck him dead for his sins, he could not imagine. Before he left his room the following morning two things were clear to Gardiner. First, it could not be long before God dealt with him as he deserved, and, secondly, while he remained on this side of hell, he would strive in some feeble measure to bring glory to the God whom he had so deeply offended. The thought that there might be pardon for his sins was as yet far from his mind. . . .

For three months Gardiner remained in this condition. Only then did he begin to entertain some hope that forgiveness was possible even to so grievous an offender as he had been. At the end of October 1719, God granted an assurance of pardon which flooded his whole being with joy. It came as he read the words of Romans 3:25-26—words to be forever written in shining letters in his experience: "Christ Jesus . . . whom God hath set forth to be a propitiation through faith in his blood, to declare his righteousness for the remission of sins that are past, through the forbearance of God."

Ecstatic with joy, James Gardiner, now thirty-one years of age, could scarcely contain his happiness. For three nights sleep eluded him as he felt "the rapturous experience of that joy unspeakable and full of glory which seemed to overflow his very soul." . . . The first to learn of his conversion was his mother, whose faithful prayers had followed her only remaining son throughout his years of ungodly living.[1]

the Father after being raised from the dead. When the Father exalted the resurrected Christ by placing Him at His right hand, He verified that Christ's claims were true—He declared Christ's righteousness. And the Holy Spirit takes this truth and convicts men that Christ's claims are true, especially His claim to be the only way of salvation.

Finally, the Holy Spirit convicts the person that there is a judgment coming for rejecting the gospel message. When Christ died on the cross, He judged the prince of this world; He crushed the serpent's head. As I have heard someone say before, "He dealt Satan a knockout punch." Because Satan has been judged by the cross and will receive his final punishment in the end, the unbeliever can be sure that he too will receive judgment if he remains on Satan's side.

These three areas of conviction are the gospel message. It is the message that the Spirit uses to convict men. Simply put, the Spirit proves to the sinner that he is wrong, that Christ can save him, and that all who are not saved will be judged. We should praise our Holy Spirit that He has not left us to ourselves. He was gracious enough to convict us of our need for Christ.

Regeneration

If a person receives the conviction of the Spirit and believes the Spirit's witness to Christ, then the Spirit regenerates him. Paul refers to this work when he commends the Thessalonians for repenting and believing the Word (I Thess. 1:5-6). From this passage and others, we know that repentance and faith are the required responses to the conviction of the Spirit and the necessary antecedents to regeneration. Though we may talk of faith and regeneration as separate events, they are simultaneous in time. A person believes and is regenerated in an instant.

What Is Regeneration?

Regeneration is *the Holy Spirit's giving to the believing sinner a new nature.* It begins to restore the image of God in the believer and to change him into Christ's likeness. When Adam fell in the Garden, the image of God in man was marred by sin. It's not until man is regenerated that the image of God begins to be restored. This restoration culminates when the believer is glorified and all the effects of sin are removed from him. He will be completely changed into Christ's image. Though man would like to believe he can change himself, he cannot. Regeneration is solely the work of God, not of man (John 1:12-13); more specifically, it is the work of the Holy Spirit (John 6:63; II Cor. 3:6-8; Titus 3:5).

> *Regeneration is solely the work of God.*

In Galatians 3 Paul makes it clear that regeneration is received through faith (3:2, 3, 5, 14). He also states that if believers receive the Spirit by faith, then it is logical that they must also grow and walk in the Spirit by faith (5:25). We must believe and trust in God to do what we cannot do. Once we believe, God the Spirit gives us a new nature, a nature that has characteristics of the divine nature. That is the reason that Peter states we have become "partakers" of the divine nature (II Pet. 1:4). What are the divine characteristics of the new nature? They are primarily two.

Eternal Life

First and foremost, we receive eternal life (Gal. 6:8). In many ways, eternal life is the essence of regeneration. No doubt you've heard John 3:16 read or quoted many times in your life, and you can probably quote it from memory yourself. But do you really know what everlasting life, or eternal life, is? Take out a piece of paper and write your own definition of eternal life. When you finish, read the next paragraph.

In John 17:1-3, Christ explains what eternal life is in His intercessory prayer for us: "Father, the hour is come; glorify thy Son, that thy Son also may glorify thee: As thou hast given him power over all flesh, that he should give eternal life to as many as thou hast given him. And this is life eternal, that they might know thee the only true God, and Jesus Christ, whom thou hast sent." Jesus Christ states that eternal life is *knowing God.* It is the restored ability to commune with, fellowship with, and enjoy God. That is true life! The world thinks that life consists of experiences, events, and entertainment—in other words, "living it up." But these pursuits do not bring satisfaction.

True life is being satisfied with the knowledge of God. It's growing closer to Him. The possession of this quality is truly divine. Christ possesses it; the Father and He are one and enjoy eternal fellowship. The Christian also—because the Spirit has given him eternal life—can know and commune with the living God. The experience of knowing God will last for all of eternity in heaven. Experiencing heaven will be experiencing God. What knowledge that will be in heaven, when we get to behold Him face to face (I Cor. 13:12)! Our hearts should cry out today for a fuller experience of God. If you have been saved, have you praised God the Spirit for giving you eternal life?

Spiritual Freedom

The second characteristic of the new nature is the freedom to do good—in will, intellect, and emotion. Liberty has two sides. On one side, liberty is releasing a person from bondage; on the other, liberty is granting a person some type of ability or privilege. Biblically speaking, the Spirit liberates the believer from his sin and grants him the ability to serve God: "But now being made free from sin, and become servants to God, ye have your fruit unto holiness, and the end everlasting life" (Rom. 6:22). If you are a Christian, you can now say no to sin. Before regeneration, you were enslaved to your sins. You were a child of the flesh like Ishmael, not a child of the Spirit like Isaac (Gal. 4:29).

Your thoughts were evil, your choices were evil, and your emotions were evil. But now the Spirit gives you a nature that is capable of reflecting God's holiness. You don't have to sin! If Christians would grasp this concept, there would be great liberty. For "where the Spirit of the Lord is, there is liberty" (II Cor. 3:17). What amazing blessings are ours even in the initial work of the Spirit!

The Role of the Bible in Regeneration

The Word of God is very important in regeneration. So much so that Peter tells us that we were "born again . . . by the word of God, which liveth and abideth for ever" (I Pet. 1:23). As mentioned before, the Holy Spirit's ordained means of convicting a person and bringing him to faith is the Word of God. No one was

ever saved apart from it. In that sense, all Christians were born of the Word of God. Paul states in Romans, "Faith cometh by hearing, and hearing by the word of God" (Rom. 10:17). A person cannot express faith in Jesus Christ unless he accepts what the Bible reveals about Him. He must hear and believe the Word of God in order to be regenerated. A good illustration of this truth is found in John 3, perhaps the most famous conversation recorded in the Bible.

John 3—Nicodemus and Regeneration

"What? That's ridiculous! How can a grown man go back into his mother's womb and be born again?" exclaimed the befuddled Pharisee. His name was Nicodemus, and his midnight conversation with Jesus provides us with the Bible's greatest text on regeneration. What is amazing to me about Nicodemus's story was not so much that he misunderstood regeneration but that he was supposed to be a teacher of it. How would you like to have been one of his students? That's like going to get white-water kayaking lessons from a supposed expert, only to find that he doesn't know what a kayak is. Christ Himself was amazed that Nicodemus did not understand regeneration: "Art thou a master of Israel, and knowest not these things?" But despite Nicodemus's surprising ignorance, his conversation with the Lord teaches us valuable lessons about regeneration. They are as follows:

All Christians were born of the Word of God.

1. Regeneration is a necessity for entering God's kingdom. Nobody will see God unless he has a new nature (v. 3).

2. Regeneration is supernatural. It is not something that man can do for himself or for another person. Regeneration is a work of God the Spirit (v. 5).

3. Regeneration concerns a person's spiritual being, not his physical being. The Spirit works in man's spirit (v. 6).

4. Regeneration itself is unseen; however, its effects are seen. Christ was teaching in John 3:8 that just as the wind's blowing is invisible, so also is the work of the Spirit. You cannot see the wind, but you hear its sound—its rustling of the leaves or twirling of the branches. Likewise, you do not see the Holy Spirit regenerating a person, but you see the results—the person's altered thoughts and ways. How has the Spirit changed your life?

5. Regeneration occurred in the lives of Old Testament saints. Christ expected that Nicodemus, as a teacher of the law, would have learned about regeneration by reading the Old Testament. Thus the Holy Spirit was certainly performing this work in the lives of Old Testament saints.

6. Regeneration is received through faith. The best-known verse in the Bible, John 3:16, teaches that a person receives everlasting life through faith. Since eternal life is the essence of regeneration and eternal life is given only to those who believe, regeneration must follow faith. Christ was telling Nicodemus that he must believe in order to receive the new birth.

Conclusion

Summarizing the work of regeneration, Charles Ryrie writes, "One may put it all together this way. God regenerates (John 1:13) according to His will (James 1:18) through the sovereign work of the Holy Spirit (John 3:5) when a person believes (John 1:12 [John 3:16]) the gospel as revealed in the Word of God (I Peter 1:23)." We truly can stand amazed in the presence of God the Spirit and render worship to Him for His wondrous grace. The complexity of just this one facet of salvation can baffle the greatest theologian and yet comfort the vilest sinner. Praise the Holy Spirit that He has given us a new nature so that we may commune with God and be free to serve Him.

End Notes

[1]Faith Cook, *Sound of Trumpets* (London: Banner of Truth, 2000). Pages 3-9. Used by permission.

Review Questions

1. What do we mean when we say that the Holy Spirit convicts of righteousness?

2. Why do people sometimes say that when a person is saved he is a *new man?*

3. Can a person fellowship with God before he is regenerated? Why or why not?

4. Why did Christ use the illustration of wind in connection with regeneration?

5. Evaluate the following statement: Conviction is the deep-rooted feeling of sorrow for doing wrong.

6. How does understanding regeneration help a Christian in his struggle to overcome sin?

"He is good; for His loving loyalty endures forever," sang out the priestly singers, accompanied by cymbals, harps, lyres, and one hundred twenty trumpets. They sounded with one voice to praise and glorify Jehovah. And as they finished their doxology, the glory of the Lord descended and filled the temple. So much so, they had to leave where they were standing lest they be consumed. Jehovah was in their midst.

It was then that Solomon opened his mouth in his dedicatory prayer for the temple. With brilliant words and phrases, he extolled the nature and works of God. When he finished, fire flashed and darted down from heaven, consuming the burnt offerings and the sacrifices. Seeing the fire fall in such splendor, everyone bowed down to the ground and echoed the Levitical singers: "He is good; for His loving loyalty is everlasting."

These events are recorded for us in II Chronicles 5 through 7. The temple of the Lord was finally completed, and the people joined together for its dedication. Although there were many lessons that the Lord was teaching the people through the temple and its services, one lesson was that His Spirit abides with His people. Just as He descended to dwell within the temple, so also He dwells with those who have been regenerated. In the New Testament age, the temple of the Holy Spirit is the believer's body. But before we look at what that involves, we need to look at more biblical evidence concerning indwelling.

What Is the Spirit's Indwelling?

Indwelling Defined

Very simply, indwelling refers to *the Holy Spirit's residing within the body of the believer.* God is in you if you are a Christian. That's a statement that boggles the mind, but Scripture clearly teaches this truth. Paul states, "Know ye not that ye are the temple of God, and that the Spirit of God dwelleth in you?" (I Cor. 3:16). Second Timothy 1:14 says, "That good thing which was committed unto thee keep by the Holy Ghost which dwelleth in us." And Peter tells the persecuted Christians that their reproach is proof of the Spirit's indwelling: "If ye be reproached for the name of Christ, happy are ye; for the Spirit of glory and of God resteth upon you" (I Pet. 4:14). All of these references point to the fact that the Spirit dwells within saved individuals.

Indwelling Defended

Some Christians have asked, "Can I lose the Holy Spirit's indwelling?" The answer is a definite "No"; your sin cannot make the Spirit leave. The Holy Spirit permanently abides within every believer, even if he has sin in his life. When Paul wrote

You are His temple.

that Christians are the temple of the Holy Ghost, he was writing to carnal, sinning Christians. What is affected by sin is the influence of the Spirit. A believer cannot cause His presence to leave him, but sin does quench the Spirit's influence on a believer's life and invokes chastisement from God.

If the Spirit does not dwell in you, you do not belong to Christ. Romans 8:9 states, "But ye are not in the flesh, but in the Spirit, if so be that the Spirit of God dwell in you. Now if any man have not the Spirit of Christ, he is none of his." This verse gives a solemn warning: to be without the Spirit is to be without salvation. But if the Spirit has regenerated you, then He also indwells you. You are His temple.

This truth, however, needs to be balanced with the reality that some who profess salvation may not be saved. The Bible gives a clear and solemn warning in Hebrews 6 about those who seem to be saved outwardly but are not inwardly: "For it is impossible for those who were once enlightened, and have tasted of the heavenly gift, and were made partakers of the Holy Ghost, and have tasted the good word of God, and the powers of the world to come, if they shall fall away, to renew them again unto repentance; seeing they crucify to themselves the Son of God afresh, and put him to an open shame." Many of these descriptions give the appearance of true conversion, but none of them actually describes a true believer. Notice that the writer never uses the word "saint" or "believer" to describe them. These people are merely going through the motions of outward church life without ever truly believing in

Christ. One phrase bears particular significance for our discussion, since it would seem to indicate that the Spirit's indwelling is not permanent for believers. It is the phrase "were made partakers of the Holy Ghost." These words, however, do not describe a true believer. Rather, they describe a person to whom the Spirit ministered to some degree, but who was never indwelt. It describes someone like Judas.

Judas was made a "partaker" of the Holy Spirit. He repeatedly saw the conviction of the Holy Spirit fall on others. He saw men

Balaam: Another Solemn Warning

Was Balaam an Old Testament believer since he experienced the power of the Spirit to prophesy? To answer that question, we have to look at the New Testament verdict on Balaam's life. We find him mentioned in three key passages. In Revelation 2:14, God condemns Balaam as someone who taught false doctrine, particularly idolatry and fornication. Both Peter and Jude identify Balaam as having gone the way to damnation (II Pet. 2:15 and Jude 11). From these passages, it is clear that Balaam was not a regenerated person. He was an unsaved man with a reputation for witchcraft and bribery. But do you remember Balaam's role in Israel's history?

When the Israelites were getting ready to cross through Moab, Balak hired Balaam to smite them with a curse (Num. 22). He did not want them to go through his land and attempted to prevent their crossing. God intervened, however, and redirected Balaam to bless Israel. Although Balak was furious, Balaam could not do otherwise. The Holy Spirit was *overpowering* him. Whereas the Spirit empowers a believer to do God's will in accordance with the believer's will, the Spirit overpowers unregenerate men who will not bow to the Spirit. Balaam serves as an example of someone who was overpowered by the Spirit to accomplish God's will.

Before we leave Balaam's story, though, I would like to point out something that is often overlooked. Do you realize that Balaam had probably the greatest amount of truth given to him to repent in the Old Testament? When we think of God's miraculous intervention to save a man in the New Testament, we immediately go to Saul of Tarsus. Jesus spoke to him directly from heaven in a glorious vision, and Saul believed. Balaam didn't, and he experienced direct intervention from all three persons of the Trinity! In Numbers 22, God the Father directly spoke to him concerning the nation of Israel

(22:9-12, 20). When he purposed to go with the Moabites, Christ appeared as the Angel of the Lord to prevent Balaam (22:22-35). And in 24:2-9, the Spirit overpowered him to prevent his speaking of a curse. Still Balaam did not turn to serve the living God. In the end, he was slain with the rest of the Moabites (Josh. 13:22), and his name represents those who serve the Lord out of false motives and desires (II Pet. 2:15; Jude 11; Rev. 2:14). He is also a warning for you today if you are serving the Lord for false motives and reasons. If you are like Balaam—a man who knew the right way but rejected it inwardly—your end will be the same. God judges all who turn away from Him.

and women regenerated and their lives dramatically changed. He knew that Christ was empowered by the Spirit to do His miracles. Judas was even used by the Holy Spirit to cast out demons and to heal the sick. Yet despite all of this, he never believed. He was as close to the Savior as a person can get, but he never expressed true faith. In the end, he went out from among the disciples because he never truly was one (I John 2:19).

What is striking about Judas's life, though, is that he was never suspected by the other disciples. When Christ announced that someone would betray Him, they argued among themselves about who it would be. No one turned around and pointed to Judas. In fact, even when Jesus directly pointed to Judas and sent him away, the disciples still did not have a clue. They assumed he was going out to buy something, not to sell someone. Judas blended in well with the other disciples without ever repenting and believing. He knew the talk and how to walk, but he never knew the Savior. Does his life describe you?

Why Does the Spirit Indwell Us?

Fellowship with God

There are two major purposes for the indwelling of the Spirit. First, the Spirit indwells believers so that they may have close fellowship with God. (It is in fellowship that we see a very close link in the purposes of regeneration and indwelling. You cannot have one without the other.) The Christian can always be assured of His presence. That abiding presence is one of the most comforting realities for the Christian. If you are saved, the Spirit can minister to you no matter where you are. Whether you are on the peaks of the Alps or in the depths of the Pacific, whether you are on the sands of the Sahara or in the fields of Nebraska, whether you are at school in the locker room or at home in the bedroom, God the Spirit is with you to minister to your spirit. The more aware that Christians are of this reality, the more they will gain in their communion with God. How aware are you of God's Spirit? If you are a Christian, have you really contemplated what it means to be indwelled by God?

Fellowship with Christians

Second, the Spirit indwells believers in order that they might experience unity. In Ephesians 4:3 Paul exhorts the believers to maintain the unity of the Spirit in the bond of peace. He also writes in Philippians 2:1-4 that if there is going to be the fellowship of the Spirit, believers must do things in humility, not through "strife" or "vainglory." Whereas unbelievers are characterized by strife—each person seeking to advance above the others—Christians are to strive for peaceful harmony.

Whereas unbelievers are characterized by strife . . . Christians are to strive for peaceful harmony.

That unity is possible because Christians are all indwelt by one Spirit and He unifies them in their spirits. He is promoting the kingdom of God, which is righteousness, peace, and joy in the Holy Spirit (Rom. 14:17). But true peace and harmony can be realized only if Christians are seeking the fellowship of the Spirit and basing their unity on what He deems important.

One church that had a problem with unity was the Corinthian church. Paul closes his second epistle to them by expressing his desire for the Corinthians to experience greater harmony. He writes, "The grace of the Lord Jesus Christ, and the love of God, and the communion of the Holy Ghost, be with you all. Amen" (II Cor. 13:14). Paul expressed the three character traits that the Corinthians needed most if they were to live in the unity of the Spirit.

Second Corinthians gives us an example of two believers dwelling in unity because of the Spirit; they are Paul and Titus. Before being regenerated and indwelled, Paul never would have held any Gentile in esteem. Paul was a Hebrew of Hebrews, a Pharisee; he was known for advancing above his contemporaries. In contrast, Titus was an uncircumcised Gentile. But because they were indwelled by the same Spirit, these men sought to minister to the Corinthians in the same way. In fact, Paul and Titus's unity and sameness of walk was a testimony and a pattern for the Corinthians to follow (II Cor. 12:18). As the psalmist said hundreds of years earlier, "Behold, how good and how pleasant it is for brethren to dwell together in unity" (Ps. 133:1).

Sometimes Christians can forget that there is more to the Christian life than just defending against wrong doctrine and separating from false teachers. If two people have been saved and are walking according to the Bible, there is no reason for their fellowship to be hindered. If it is being hindered, the cause may be pride. All believers are sinners saved by grace. And because that is true, the rich can fellowship with the poor, the educated with the uneducated, the outgoing with the shy, the prominent with the unknown, and so on. The Spirit is seeking to unify the body of Christ. Looking down on others hinders the communion that should characterize all Christians. Learn to fellowship with other believers.

What Are the Implications of the Spirit's Indwelling?

The New Testament gives several implications of the Spirit's indwelling. These implications are sometimes given explicitly and sometimes implicitly by analogy, particularly the analogy of the believer's body to the temple. In fact, Paul uses the imagery of the temple repeatedly in Corinthians to describe the Spirit's indwelling of the believer. It is a beautiful analogy with powerful lessons.

Lessons from the Temple

1. **You belong to God, not yourself.** Paul makes this application in I Corinthians 6:19-20: "What? know ye not that your body is the temple of the Holy Ghost which is in you, which ye have of God, and ye are not your own? For ye are bought with a price: therefore glorify God in your body, and in your spirit, which are God's." The temple of

God never belonged to any man. It didn't even belong to the nation of Israel; it was God's possession. Solomon's dedicatory prayer made this clear: "For the palace [temple] is not for man, but for the Lord God" (I Chron. 29:1).

2. **Your body must glorify God.** To glorify God means to *call attention to God.* If you glorify someone, you are lifting up that person in honor for who he is or what he has done. If your body is God's, then you must use it to call attention to God. Your temple must highlight His attributes and works. How is this glorification accomplished? By using your body for the worship and service of God, just as the temple was used in the Old Testament. All of the temple's vessels contributed to the service of God. Psalm 29:9 states, "And in his temple doth every one speak of his glory." So if your body is God's temple, all of your bodily members must be used to glorify Him.

A Common Bond

Think About It!

Have you ever walked into a restaurant and seen another family or couple pray before eating? Though you may have never met the people before, you could sense a connection with them. You realize that despite peripheral differences, you both have the same Lord and the same Spirit. In fact, you might even have more in common with these "strangers" than you do with your own unsaved relatives. That commonality is a blessing of the Spirit's indwelling.

3. **You must keep your temple holy.** Holiness is the central attribute that we are to call attention to. After stating that our bodies are God's temple, Paul writes, "For the temple of God is holy, which temple ye are" (I Cor. 3:16-17). Knowing that the Holy Spirit demands absolute purity for His habitation should compel you to keep yourself clean and pure. You should allow your mind to feast only on thoughts that are pure and true. You must use your body for works of righteousness and goodness. Paul gives a fearful warning in this passage for those who do not: "If any man defile the temple of God, him shall God destroy." That statement leads to one final aspect of holiness.

4. **You must not defile the temple.** In the Old Testament, a person could defile the temple by bringing in something that was unholy or idolatrous. For example, the wicked king Manasseh brought pagan altars and idols into the temple, and he worshiped false gods there (II Kings 21). He allowed immoral and ungodly practices to happen within the temple of God. And so can you. By allowing your mind to take in immoral scenes from the TV, you are defiling the temple of God. If you harbor sins within your heart, you are dirtying His holy habitation. Though your temple may look clean outwardly,

If your body is God's temple, all of your bodily members must be used to glorify Him.

it could be housing thoughts that are unclean. If that is so, you should confess those sins now and clean out the temple that is intended for God's glory. By God's grace, you can restore your temple to its correct use. Manasseh did. After the Lord humbled him and allowed him to be exiled to Babylon, he repented of his sins and was saved. Thereafter, he took away all of the idols and altars that he had set up in the temple (II Chron. 33:15).

The second way that a person can defile the temple is by using its vessels improperly. Belshazzar used the temple vessels for his immoral feast to a false god (Dan. 5). He employed the utensils that were dedicated to God's service for selfish and ungodly purposes. Likewise, you can take your temple vessels and use them wrongly as well. By stealing with your hands, singing sensually with your voice, or using your talents to advance yourself, you are using God's temple vessels improperly. But God's vessels are for His use only. Are you using your temple vessels for His glory?

Keeping the Temple in Shape

In light of these four lessons from the temple, what would you say to a fellow Christian who did not exercise regularly and regularly overate? Do you think that these truths apply to our maintaining a healthy body?

Think About It!

Review Questions

1. Why do you think that the Levites hurried away when the Lord's presence descended on the temple?

2. Do you think that somebody who hasn't been regenerated can be indwelled by the Spirit? Why or why not?

3. Apart from the examples listed in the text, how else could a person defile his temple?

4. How should the knowledge that God owns the believer's temple (body) change the way a believer lives?

5. Suppose that two campers are assigned the same cabin during their week at camp. They are both Christians, but they disagree sharply concerning whether or not someone should be home schooled. How should they act toward one another? What are some verses that you would use to direct their behavior?

6. Read the story of Jonathan and David in I Samuel 18:1-5, 19:1-7, and 20:1-42. What examples of unity do they show? What reasons might they have had to disagree and be angry with each other?

I will never forget that excruciating feeling. As I lay on the floor of the supermarket's break room, I was slowly being overtaken by severe pain in my abdomen. Having had some informal training in the medical area, I knew precisely what was wrong. I had appendicitis—bad. My mom picked me up from the grocery store and rushed me to the emergency room of the hospital. By then I was doubled over in pain and fighting the tears.

A doctor examined me and patronizingly asserted that I was experiencing a "tummy ache" from something I had eaten that morning. *If he only knew how much pain I was in,* I thought. *Eighteen-year-old guys do not ask their moms to take them to the emergency room for "tummy aches."* Fighting my carnal impulse to get angry, I instead politely asked that he take some x-rays. He reluctantly complied and gave instructions for the procedure.

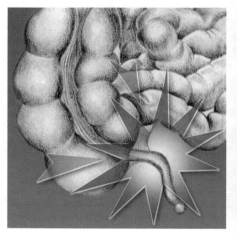

Within a few minutes after the x-rays, he was rushing back into my room and barking orders for an immediate surgery. My appendix was double the normal size and had flipped upside down; it was ready to explode. "Boy," he remarked, "you've got to be in some pretty unbearable pain." I winced. There weren't any feelings left to feel angry or smug. I just wanted to be painless.

During the next few weeks as I recovered, I often contemplated the wonder of the body. Each organ, muscle, bone, or tissue does its part. It's not until you damage or break one of these parts that you really begin to appreciate even the smallest members of your body.

Take your toes, for example. They're small, unattractive, and seem rather unimportant. But stub one of those little fellas on a chair and you can hardly walk. Or consider your eye. It measures barely five centimeters in diameter. But get a speck of sawdust in it and you won't be able to finish work or even drive home. Damage both of them and you may never see correctly again.

The body fascinates us not just because of each member's importance but also because of the connection between the members. The intricate cardiovascular system still challenges the most intelligent doctor. All the parts of the system—the heart, aortas, veins, capillaries, platelets, red blood cells, white blood cells, and

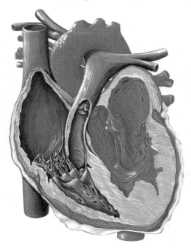

more—work together beautifully; they pump blood to the whole body. The cardiovascular system cannot work alone, though. It also relies on other systems. And those systems work with other systems that are just as complicated, and they all do so in complete harmony. It's no wonder, then, that the Bible uses the imagery of a body to illustrate how Christians are to relate to each other in the church. All Christians are part of the body of Christ. We become part of His body through the Spirit's work of baptism.

What Is Spirit Baptism?

The baptism of the Spirit is *the Holy Spirit's placing the believer into the body of Christ at the moment of salvation.* The Spirit unites the believer with Christ, and he becomes part of Christ's body, the church. (In an extended metaphor, Paul also calls the church a temple [Eph. 2:22]). Without this baptism, we are not part of His body or under His direct authority. The passage that explains this most clearly is I Corinthians 12:13: "For by one Spirit are we all baptized into one body, whether we be Jews or Gentiles, whether we be bond or free; and have been all made to drink into one Spirit." This passage teaches that Christians are baptized by the Holy Spirit. At first this may seem to contradict John the Baptist's teaching, namely that Jesus would baptize us with the Holy Spirit: "I indeed have baptized you with water: but he shall baptize you with the Holy Ghost" (Mark 1:8; see also Matt. 3:11; Luke 3:16; and John 1:33). However, if we consider all of the passages together, we realize that Christ will baptize us by the Holy Spirit into His body. Christ is the agent of the baptizing, and the Spirit is the instrument. Both are actively involved in the action. Here's a hypothetical story to illustrate the point:

> A teenager is hired by a subcontractor who is working for the Porsche company. The subcontractor promises to pay him $50 an hour to teach the Porsche employees how to correctly do a U-turn while driving 150 miles per hour on the Autobahn. The day before payday, Porsche gives the subcontractor $100,000 to cover the subcontractor's expenses. The subcontractor deposits the money into a withdrawing account, figures out how much the teenager has earned, and writes him a check for the correct amount. From whom is the teenager earning his money? Depending on your viewpoint, you could say that Porsche is paying him or, just as accurately, that the subcontractor is paying him.

Likewise, when we speak of the baptism of the Spirit, we can accurately say that Christ is the person who baptizes us or that the Holy Spirit is the one who baptizes us. However, because the Spirit specifically carries out the action of baptism, we say that it is a work of the Spirit. He directly places us into Christ's body.

We also have to understand that the Holy Spirit baptizes the believer instantaneously at the moment of salvation. Whenever Paul speaks about the baptism of the Spirit, he refers to it as something that all Christians have received. Either you are saved and in the body of Christ or you are not saved and not in the body of Christ; but you cannot be in the body of Christ and be waiting for the baptism of the Spirit. That is illogical. Some preachers falsely claim that the baptism of the Spirit is a "second blessing." Contrary to their claims, though, the Spirit places the believer into the body of Christ once and for all. Careful interpreting of Scripture will dispel the clouds of misunderstanding. We will examine the teaching about Spirit baptism in the Gospels, in the book of Acts, and in the Epistles.

The Spirit places the believer into the body of Christ once and for all.

Spirit Baptism in the Gospels

Each Gospel mentions the baptism of the Spirit only one time, and they all do so in the same context. In Matthew 3:11 John the Baptist states that whereas he baptized with water, there would be one who would baptize with the Holy Ghost and fire. Mark 1:8 and Luke 3:16 record similar statements. In the Gospel of John, however, we find out how John knew about the future baptism of the Spirit. God the Father revealed it to him. "Upon whom thou shalt see the Spirit descending, and remaining on him, the same is he which baptizeth with the Holy Ghost" (John 1:33). These verses teach that the spiritual baptism by the Spirit was going to be a new ministry, a ministry previously unknown.

Spirit Baptism in Acts

In Acts 1:4-5 Luke records for us some of the last words of Christ before His ascension. Christ was speaking to His disciples, and, "being assembled together with them, commanded them that they should not depart from Jerusalem, but wait for the promise of the Father, which, saith he, ye have heard of me. For John truly baptized with water; but ye shall be baptized with the Holy Ghost not many days hence." The baptism of the Spirit was still a future event. In Acts 2, though, they were no longer waiting.

On the day of Pentecost, the disciples and other believers were gathered together in one place. Suddenly, the Holy Ghost descended upon them and baptized all of them, accompanied by outward symbols and signs. The news spread quickly, and soon the disciples were standing before thousands of people, speaking and teaching in other tongues. Peter, the leader of the disciples, stood up and explained what was happening. He demonstrated from Joel 2 that the baptism of the Spirit had happened: God had poured out His Spirit upon all flesh (Acts 2:17-18). And in order to receive this baptism, one must submit to the Lord Jesus Christ in salvation (2:38).

At this point, only Jews were present (Acts 2:5). But remember, the baptism of the Spirit is not exclusive to Jews. It is for all peoples. Christ brings both Jew and Gentile into one body and unifies them. The Jews were the first of four groups to be confronted with these truths, and many of them believed and were baptized.

The second group was the Samaritans—the despised Israelites who lived northeast of Jerusalem. The Samaritans worshiped in Mt. Gerizim rather than Jerusalem. They were half Jewish because of the forced immigration of foreigners by Assyria after Samaria fell in 722 B.C. For those two reasons the Samaritans and Jews loathed each other. They both needed to learn unity. So when we find Philip preaching to the Samaritans in Acts 8, we know that something unusual and splendid is about to happen. Philip gives the Samaritans the gospel of Christ, and many believe his word and

are baptized by water (8:12). When the apostles in Jerusalem hear that the Samaritans have believed, they immediately come to Samaria. They pray and lay their hands on the Samaritans, and the Samaritans are baptized into the body of Christ. Two groups of people who have hated each other for centuries are now one body of believers.

Two groups down; two to go. But before we look at the other two groups, I would like to answer a question that is commonly raised concerning this passage.

Why did the Samaritans have to wait to receive the baptism of the Spirit by the apostles in Acts 8:15-17? The Samaritans needed to wait because they needed to learn a powerful lesson: they were no longer to have a separate worship center or separate way of worshiping. The church of Christ is to be unified with Christ as its head. To show them this lesson, God brought the apostles from Jerusalem to Samaria. By placing their hands on the Samaritans, the apostles were demonstrating the authority that Christ had given them as apostles, and they were teaching the Samaritans to be unified with their Jewish brethren.

The third group of people to be brought into the body of Christ was the Gentiles. The Gentiles received the baptism of the Spirit in Acts 10 when Peter went to preach to Cornelius. Before he preached, though, God had to teach Peter that the Gentiles were not to be regarded as unclean anymore. Peter's vision of the white sheet with unclean animals prepared him for what was about to happen. As soon as the vision had ended, three men knocked on the door and asked Peter to come to Cornelius. Peter obeyed the Spirit's command and went (10:19-23). After he preached the gospel of Christ and the Gentiles believed, the Holy

Spirit descended on them as well, and they were baptized in the Spirit (10:44). They were subsequently baptized in water, as the Jews marveled at their salvation (10:45-47). At the Jerusalem Council, Peter testified that God gave the Gentiles the Holy Spirit, authenticating their conversion (Acts 15:8). God was accomplishing what had seemed impossible. Jews and Gentiles were being united in one body. Jews, Samaritans, and Gentiles were learning that salvation is in one name and that unity is through one Spirit. Only one group still needed to learn this lesson—the remaining disciples of John the Baptist.

In Acts 19:1-7 Paul comes across some disciples of John the Baptist in Ephesus. With a few questions, Paul figures out why they haven't received the baptism of the Spirit yet. Their conversation is briefly recorded in verses 2 through 4.

Paul:	"Have ye received the Holy Ghost since ye believed?"
John's disciples:	"We have not so much as heard whether there be any Holy Ghost."
Paul:	"Unto what were ye baptized?"
John's disciples:	"Unto John's baptism."
Paul:	"John verily baptized with the baptism of repentance, saying unto the people, that they should believe on him which should come after him, that is, on Christ Jesus."

Paul realizes that these men were still following John the Baptist and that they had not followed his instruction to submit to Christ Jesus. He explains that they need to come into submission to Christ and believe on Him. When they do so, Paul lays his hands on them and the Holy Spirit baptizes them into the body of Christ. They are now under Christ's headship, not John the Baptist's, and the body of Christ is now complete. All the groups understand that in Christ's body Christ alone is head. From this time on, Spirit baptism occurs simultaneously with salvation. It is no longer mentioned in the book of Acts as something to wait for.

GET THE BIG PICTURE

Recipients of Spirit Baptism

The baptism of the Spirit incorporates Jews.	Acts 2
The baptism of the Spirit incorporates Samaritans.	Acts 8
The baptism of the Spirit incorporates Gentiles.	Acts 10 and 11
The baptism of the Spirit incorporates John's disciples.	Acts 19

Spirit Baptism in the Epistles

I Corinthians

What Luke chronicles in Acts, Paul elucidates plainly in his epistles. He teaches precisely what happens at Spirit baptism. Now that you have seen the four accounts of Spirit baptism in Acts, you will undoubtedly understand and appreciate Paul's clear explanation in I Corinthians 12:13: "For by one Spirit are we all baptized into one body, whether we be Jews or Gentiles, whether we be bond or free; and have been all made to drink into one Spirit." Paul, knowing that all groups are under the dominion of Christ, can write assuredly that if you are saved you have been baptized into the body of Christ. Just as all Christians have one Lord and one faith, so also they have been baptized by one Spirit (Eph. 4:5). In fact, Paul assumes that it has already happened to every believer reading the epistle in Corinth. That is a crucial assumption, an assumption that destroys the possibility of a "second blessing." Paul never commands a believer to be baptized by the Spirit or to wait for the baptism. The baptism of the Spirit is accomplished for every believer at the moment of salvation.

Romans

In the book of Romans, Spirit baptism is inseparably linked to our union with Christ (6:1-6). According to the teaching of the New Testament, you cannot have one without the other. Romans 6 teaches that if we have been baptized into Christ, then out of logical necessity we have also first been united with Christ. In other words, you cannot be part of the body of Christ without having been first united with Christ. That statement nullifies the Roman Catholic teaching that church membership is the basis for union with Christ. It's the other way around. A person is baptized into the body of Christ automatically when he is born again. Regeneration always results in Spirit baptism.

Also in Romans 6, Paul is strongly arguing against those who think that being in the body of Christ allows a free ticket to sinning. May it never be! If you have truly been baptized into Christ, then you should know that you have been united with Him as

Bringing It Home

Though the local church is supposed to represent a gathering of true regenerated believers, there are obviously some within the local church that are not really part of the body of Christ. They believe church membership and attendance guarantees salvation. They believe that because they go every Sunday, tithe regularly, and bring their Bibles, they are saved. But no matter how well-intentioned a person may be, God's Word is clear. The Spirit baptizes you into the body of Christ because you have been regenerated and justified by faith in Christ's work on the cross. Faith alone is necessary for salvation. Are you trusting in Jesus Christ alone for your salvation? You cannot rely on any amount of "Christian" service to bring you to salvation and to give you peace. You must trust in Christ. If you haven't, will you do it today?

well. Therefore, your old self has been crucified and you have a new nature that desires to serve Christ. You are no longer a slave to sin. Your new Master is the Lord Jesus Christ.

Galatians

In Galatians Paul argues indirectly that the baptism of the Spirit happens at the time of salvation through faith. "But before faith came, we were kept under the law, shut up unto the faith which should afterwards be revealed. Wherefore the law was our schoolmaster to bring us unto Christ, that we might be justified by faith. But after that faith is come, we are no longer under a schoolmaster. For ye are all the children of God by faith in Christ Jesus" (Gal. 3:23-28). According to this passage, being baptized into the body of Christ happens with justification at salvation. To separate the baptism of the Spirit from the time of justification would directly contradict these verses.

Ephesians

In the book of Ephesians Paul teaches that Christ is the head of the body. He is the body's authority, and all the members must submit to Him. This submission is the Father's will: "He [the Father] . . . hath put all things under his feet, and gave him to be the head over all things to the church, which is his body, the fulness of him that filleth all in all" (1:22-23). Paul teaches that the church must follow the headship of Christ. He is the ruler of His people. Paul also reveals the mystery of Christ that was hidden for ages, namely "that the Gentiles should be fellowheirs, and of the same body, and partakers of his promise in Christ by the gospel" (3:6). Because the Spirit baptism has been finally realized, believing Gentiles are part of the body of Christ. Every believer, despite race, color, or background, is part of one body in Christ. To become part of the body, you must believe in the gospel of Christ. Have you received the gospel and been baptized into His body? Are you living under Christ's authority?

What Are the Blessings of Being Baptized into Christ's Body?

When the Holy Spirit baptizes a believer into the body of Christ, He also equips the believer with spiritual capabilities. The New Testament calls these capabilities spiritual gifts. Chapter 5 will address the topic of spiritual gifts in detail.

Another key blessing accompanied the baptism of the Spirit—the possibility of Gentiles serving. That blessing should not be underestimated. According to Old Testament teaching, Gentiles

---

NT Teaching on Spirit Baptism

GET THE BIG PICTURE

1. The Gospels state that Christ would baptize with the Holy Ghost.

2. Acts records the baptism of four groups of believers. These four groups represent all the possible groups of believers.

3. The Epistles teach that baptism of the Spirit is membership within the body of Christ, not a second blessing.

4. The Epistles teach that Christ is the head of the body.

5. The Epistles assume and state that all believers are baptized by one Spirit at salvation.

6. The New Testament never commands a person to ask, wait, or pray for the baptism of the Spirit.

were not allowed to serve within the Lord's house. For example, if you were a Gentile with a wonderful voice, you still could not sing among the Levitical singers. Even if you were very knowledgeable about God's Word, you could not hold a position as a teacher of the law. Gentiles were, as Paul states, "aliens from the commonwealth of Israel, and strangers from the covenants of promise" (Eph. 2:12). Furthermore, being a Jew in Old Testament times did not necessarily guarantee that a person would be empowered by the Spirit. Generally, only leaders such as prophets, priests, and kings were empowered to do God's service. But with the baptism of the Spirit in New Testament times, even servants and slaves who were saved were empowered to speak God's Word and to minister.

That's what was truly amazing about the Spirit's baptism, and that's what dramatically distinguished the Spirit's New Testament work from His Old Testament work. Although Old Testament saints experienced the regenerating of the Holy Spirit, they never experienced the baptism of the Spirit. This work inaugurated an age unknown and unanticipated by Israel. The outpouring of the Spirit upon all flesh would mark the New Testament Church. All believers—free or bond, rich or poor, king or farmer—would be endowed with some spiritual gift and the empowerment to use that gift.

Here we may pause and marvel at the graciousness of God, that He would pour out His Spirit on us so that we too may come and worship Him with our gifts. "Unto Him be glory in the church by Christ Jesus throughout all ages, world without end"

(Eph. 3:21). The majestic redemptive plan of the Trinity can be seen at every point of salvation, including the baptism of the Spirit. May God the Father be adored for what God the Son accomplished and God the Spirit applied.

As you read the following hymn about the Trinity, focus on the points that call attention to the Holy Spirit. Also, do you know what day the author is referring to?

Think About It!

O Day of Rest and Gladness

Christopher Wordsworth

O day of rest and gladness,
    O day of joy and light,
O balm of care and sadness,
    most beautiful, most bright;
On thee the high and lowly,
    through ages joined in tune,
Sing "Holy, holy, holy,"
    to the great God Triune.

On thee, at the creation,
    the light first had its birth;
On thee, for our salvation,
    Christ rose from depths of earth;
On thee our Lord victorious,
    the Spirit sent from heaven;
And thus on thee most glorious
    a triple light was given.

Today on weary nations,
    the heavenly manna falls;
To holy convocations
    the silver trumpet calls;
Where gospel light is glowing
    with pure and radiant beams,
And living water flowing
    with soul-refreshing streams.

New graces ever gaining
    from this our day of rest,
We reach the rest remaining
    to spirits of the blest;
To Holy Ghost be praises,
    to Father and to Son;
The Church her voice upraises
    to Thee, blest Three in One.

Review Questions

1. When does a believer receive the baptism of the Spirit?

2. What passage teaches that if we have been saved we have been baptized by the Spirit?

3. Why should a Christian rejoice that he has been baptized by the Spirit?

4. Does a person need to pray for Spirit baptism? Why or why not?

5. Why had John's disciples not received the baptism of the Spirit?

6. Do you think it was hard for Philip to go preach to the Samaritans? Why or why not?

Essay

7. Tyrone attends mass at St. Mary's Church every week. When you spoke with him last time about salvation, he assured you that being part of a Roman Catholic church is the first step in getting to heaven. What would you prepare to say to him the next time that you meet?

8. Evaluate the following step-by-step procedure for "gaining the baptism of the Spirit." What verses would you use to show that this teaching is not biblical? The excerpt is taken from an actual website.

"God the Father gave (poured out) the Holy Spirit on the day of Pentecost once and for all. Therefore it is not a matter of God giving you the Holy Spirit, but rather you receiving what God has already given. Now pray to receive the Gift that God has already given to the believer. Pray the prayer of faith: Dear Lord Jesus: I thank you that you shed your blood on Calvary's cross for my sins. I ask for forgiveness for my sins and I do acknowledge you as my Lord and Savior. I ask you to baptize me in the Holy Spirit. I claim by faith the baptism in the Holy Spirit right now. Thank you Jesus, Amen. Now, begin to praise Jesus, but not in your language. You will be using your vocal cords and lips and you will be speaking as on the day of Pentecost, but the Holy Spirit will be giving you a new language to praise God. You will have another hot line to heaven with which to pray and praise the Lord."

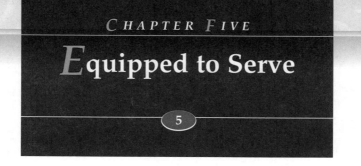

So far you have covered a lot of material. In Chapter 1, you looked at the person of the Holy Spirit and learned that He is a person and that He is God. In Chapter 2, you looked at the Spirit's work of conviction, whereby He shows the sinner his need of the gospel. You were also introduced to the work of regeneration, on which all the other works of the Spirit are founded. In Chapters 3 and 4, we discussed the Holy Spirit's indwelling and baptism of the believer. You learned that the individual Christian is the temple of the Holy Ghost and that collectively Christians are the body of Christ. In this chapter we will look at one of the blessings of being in the body of Christ—spiritual gifts.

This is a very controversial subject. Unfortunately, many have misunderstood the gifts of the Spirit and have shifted the emphasis from loving and serving one another to amazing and outdoing one another. But, as you will see, love is an absolute necessity for ministering. Love is the mortar of Christian edification; you cannot build without it.

> *Love is the mortar of Christian edification; you cannot build without it.*

This chapter must necessarily refute false teaching about spiritual gifts, but the main emphasis will be to teach what spiritual gifts are and to explain why they were given. It is my desire that when you finish this chapter you will be able to understand exactly what your spiritual gift is and how you can use it to serve God and others. To accomplish this goal, we will progress in four stages. First, we will define the term *spiritual gift.* We will then look at the four major passages that address spiritual gifts, followed by an evaluation of modern claims concerning speaking in tongues. We will finish by considering what Paul says about love—the most excellent way.

What Are Spiritual Gifts?

Spiritual Gifts Defined

A spiritual gift is *a Spirit-given ability to edify other believers to the glory of God.* Each part of that definition is important and demands closer examination.

1. **The Spirit gives these gifts.** Paul clearly emphasizes that point seven times in I Corinthians 12:4, 7-11, lest anyone would think that they could fake or produce a spiritual gift: "Now there are diversities of gifts, but the same **Spirit**. . . . But the manifestation of the **Spirit** is given to every man to profit withal. For to one is given by the **Spirit** the word of wisdom; to another the word of knowledge by the same **Spirit;** to another faith by the same **Spirit;** to another the gifts of healing by the same **Spirit**. . . . But all these worketh that one and the selfsame **Spirit,** dividing to every man severally as he will." Paul is unequivocally demonstrating that the Spirit alone gives these gifts to believers. Man does not bestow them on other men. When a person is baptized by the Spirit at salvation, the Spirit imparts to that person a spiritual gift (12:13*ff*.).

2. **Gifts are abilities—spiritual enablements.** Spiritual gifts enable Christians to minister on a spiritual level. An unsaved professor may be able to communicate knowledge, but he cannot minister spiritually to his students. That is the difference between a talent and a spiritual gift. A talent is the ability or skill to accomplish something artistically, intellectually, or physically, but it is not the ability to accomplish something spiritually for another person. In order to do that, a person must have power from the Spirit.

3. **Spiritual gifts are for the purpose of edification.** That is the initial goal of exercising gifts. Ephesians 4:12 states that Christ gave spiritual gifts for "the perfecting of the saints, for the work of the ministry, for the edifying of the body of Christ." By using spiritual gifts, Christians take part in building up other Christians and helping them

grow. Choosing not to exercise your spiritual gift robs others of spiritual nourishment. In verse 13, Paul goes on to explain how long we are to edify one another. "Till we all come in the unity of the faith, and of the knowledge of the Son of God, unto a perfect man, unto the measure of the stature of the fulness of Christ." Spiritual gifts are a means of increasing our knowledge of Christ until we are finally with Him in glory. Paul also explains another aspect of edification in verse 14: "That we henceforth be no more children, tossed to and fro, and carried about with every wind of doctrine, by the sleight of men, and cunning craftiness, whereby they lie in wait to deceive." Part of our own edification is anchoring other members in truth so that they do not fall into error. If you are a member of Christ's body, you have a responsibility to build up others. Are you?

4. **Spiritual gifts are to glorify God.** That is the ultimate goal of exercising gifts. Peter completes his brief synopsis of gifts with this purpose: "That God in all things may be glorified though Jesus Christ, to whom be praise and dominion for ever and ever. Amen" (I Pet. 4:11). Clearly the purpose of edification dovetails with the purpose of glorification. If Christ does not receive the glory, edification will be in vain.

Spiritual Gifts Explained

Romans 12:3-8

Having finished his great argument concerning salvation and the hope that believers have in Christ, Paul begins in chapter 12 to give various exhortations based on the doctrines of chapters 1-11. Within these beginning exhortations, we find a brief mention of spiritual gifts. Three observations from this passage are noteworthy. First, there are different gifts distributed, but each is important. Paul does not rank the significance of every gift. He lists seven different ones and gives instruction about the manner in which they should be used. Second, Paul calls our attention to the fact that these gifts are of grace. Spirit-given abilities are not earned or merited. They are freely given by the grace of God. Because that is true, a believer should never become proud of the gifts he possesses. Nor should he diminish or despise the gifts of others. Each gift is integral for the body's vitality.

Finally, Paul emphasizes the unity of the body along with the diversity of the gifts. Each member is contributing to the health of the body. Although each member is different and possesses different gifts, all members are to glorify the head, Jesus Christ. We are members of His body. Therefore, the exercise of gifts should give glory to Him, not to self. If a person is exercising gifts to exalt himself, you can be sure he is not obeying what God has revealed in the Bible.

I Corinthians 12-14

First Corinthians 12 through 14 gives the most extensive teaching concerning gifts. Without these three chapters, our understanding of gifts would be severely limited. Though a verse-by-verse analysis would be highly profitable, we will have to narrow our analysis to bigger units of thought. However, I suggest that you read these three chapters before going on. Let's make sure that we really know what the Bible says before we proceed to classify its assertions and make conclusions.

Major Assertion #1—Spiritual gifts have one source (12:1-11). Paul begins his treatment of spiritual gifts with a two-sided, universal truth: A person cannot curse Jesus and be regenerated, and a person cannot truly affirm Jesus' deity without being regenerated. It's that simple. So if a person dismisses Christ's deity and elevates his own teaching, you know that that person is not truly regenerated, no matter how much other truth he asserts. Paul goes on to say that although there is a diversity of gifts there is only one source—the Spirit. As was mentioned before, the Spirit alone gives the gifts. They do not come from man. These verses also affirm that every believer has at least one gift (12:11).

Major Assertion #2—Spiritual gifts should promote unity, not division (12:12-31a). Paul once again uses the analogy of a physical body to teach a spiritual reality. Just as each part of the human body performs a necessary job in order for the whole body to function correctly, so also the members of the church must perform their jobs so that the church can function. Paul asks almost sarcastically, If the whole body were an eye, where would the hearing be? Or if the whole body were an ear, where would the smelling be? I think you would be disgusted to see a giant nose sitting next to you in school. It would be freaky. Similarly, if a local

church emphasizes just one gift, it is not functioning correctly, and saints are being grossly malnourished. Also, the different members of the body should work in harmony to promote the wellness of the whole body, not to divide the body. The gifts of God were given so that "the members should have the same care one for another" (12:25). Therefore, all the members of the body rise and fall together. "Whether one member suffer, all the members suffer with it; or one member be honoured, all the members rejoice with it" (12:26). The body of Christ should comprise individual members who seek to promote unity and edification by the exercise of spiritual gifts. It should not be composed of individual members who seek to promote self by the misuse or abuse of spiritual gifts.

Major Assertion #3—Spiritual gifts must be exercised in love, the greatest necessity for edification (12:31b–13:13). (I will develop this topic more fully later in the chapter.) In 13:1-3, Paul uses hyperbole to show the absurdity of exercising gifts without love. Nobody is built up, and it profits the person nothing. He then explains what love is, or rather, what it does. Paul concludes this passage with the well-known verse: "And now abideth faith, hope, charity [love], these three; but the greatest of these is charity."

Major Assertion #4—Speaking in a different language is unprofitable when the church does not understand that language (14:1-19). Having demonstrated that all gifts are Spirit-given, all are important, and all must be exercised in love, Paul now states that it is better to prophesy so that all the church understands than to speak in tongues and have no one understand (vv. 1-5). Just as a trumpet must sound a clear, understandable note in order for the army to prepare for battle, so also a person must give clear speech in order for the church to be edified (vv. 7-9). Paul also implies that tongues are known foreign languages. According to verses 10-12, there are many different kinds of languages in the world. If a person speaks in an unknown language, he will be like a foreigner to the people. That's not the goal of spiritual gifts. Rather, believers are to seek the edification of the church (v. 12). Paul also states that he would rather utter five words in the language of the people than ten thousand in a tongue they don't understand (v. 19).

Major Assertion #5—Spiritual gifts must be governed by orderliness (14:20-40). Paul finishes chapter 14 by giving rules for the exercise of spiritual gifts. Concerning tongues, he gives three rules: (1) No more than two or three people may speak, (2) they must speak one at a time, and (3) there must be an interpreter present. Concerning prophets, he gives two rules: (1) Two or three may speak, and (2) they must speak one at a time. Concerning women, they are not permitted to speak in tongues or to prophesy in church (vv. 34-35). Throughout the chapter Paul reiterates one thought—orderliness. "God is not the author of confusion, but of peace" (v. 33), and all things must be done properly and in an orderly manner (v. 40). If these rules are obeyed, unsaved observers will fall on their faces and worship God, declaring that God is certainly indwelling the members of the church (v. 25).

Ephesians 4:8-16

Paul's teaching in Ephesians 4 adds one detail previously undiscussed. The men who possess the gifts of apostleship, prophecy, evangelism, and pastor-teacher are actually gifts themselves. Christ gives these gifted men to the church for its equipping and edifying. Though the apostle and the prophet were just for the founding of the church, the evangelist and the pastor-teacher continue with us. Christ kindly gave the church men to carry on the teaching of the Word.

I Peter 4:10-11

Peter emphasizes the glory of God. As mentioned in the definition of spiritual gifts, gifts are to be used for God's glory. Whoever exercises a gift must have an eye toward Christ. He must not use his gift for his own glory. Peter also affirms that every believer has received a gift, and that each gift belongs to

DID YOU KNOW?

A Sign for the Jews

In I Corinthians 14:21-22, Paul makes a startling assertion. Quoting Isaiah 28:11, he states that tongues were given as a sign to unbelieving Jews. The nation of Israel had turned its back on God, and God was sending men who were supernaturally empowered to speak to them in foreign languages. The tongues were a sign to Jews, signifying the dawn of the church age and authenticating the truth of the gospel. Acts 2, the record of the first occurrence of tongues, even lists the different regions from which the Jews had come. "Parthians, and Medes, and Elamites, and the dwellers in Mesopotamia, and in Judaea, and Cappadocia, in Pontus, and Asia, Phrygia, and Pamphylia, in Egypt, and in the parts of Libya about Cyrene, and strangers of Rome, Jews and proselytes, Cretes and Arabians, we do hear them speak in our tongues the wonderful works of God" (vv. 9-11). Even as they were pondering over the meaning of the tongues, Peter stood up and explained that the tongues were a sign from God concerning the gospel of Jesus Christ (vv. 12-18).

The next occurrence is in Acts 10 when Cornelius and the other Gentiles who believed spoke in tongues. Again, this gift was to signify to Jews that Gentiles were part of the new organism called the church. Peter clarifies this truth in 11:15-18. "And as I began to speak, the Holy Ghost fell on them, as on us at the beginning. Then remembered I the word of the Lord, how that he said, John indeed baptized with water; but ye shall be baptized with the Holy Ghost. Forasmuch then as God gave them the like gift as he did unto us, who believed on the Lord Jesus Christ; what was I, that I could withstand God? When they heard these things, they held their peace, and glorified God, saying, Then hath God also to the Gentiles granted repentance unto life." In both incidents Jews were present. It is logical to conclude then, both from the examples in Acts and from the teaching of I Corinthians 14:21-22, that tongues were to be exercised only in the presence of Jews, since the gift was given as a sign to them.

one of two broad categories—speaking or serving. Each person must employ his gift as a steward of God's manifold grace.

Evaluating Modern Claims of Speaking in Tongues

Although numerous groups have practiced speaking in tongues in the past century, the group that has gained the widest acceptance is the Charismatics. The Charismatic movement takes its name from the Greek word *charismata,* which means gifts. Charismatics believe that they are the only ones who take spiritual gifts seriously, and that's why they chose to name their movement essentially the "gifts movement." Not every Charismatic group holds exactly the same teaching, but there are several beliefs that are common among Charismatics. First, they teach that the gift of tongues did not cease and that it had a resurgence in the twentieth century. They also claim that the gift of tongues is evidence of true salvation and that tongues-speaking is ecstatic speech, during which the person is not cognizant of what he is saying. Finally, Charismatics allow multiple people to speak in tongues in one service and at one time, and they also permit women to speak in tongues.

Claim #1: The gift of tongues did not cease

This claim is the hardest to refute because the Bible never gives a date of cessation. However, the Bible does imply that tongues would cease with the gifts of prophecy and knowledge. In I Corinthians 13:8, Paul states that three gifts will cease: prophecy, tongues, and knowledge. The gift of prophecy (the supernatural ability to give direct revelation from God) and the gift of knowledge (the supernatural ability to receive direct revelation from

God) have unquestionably ceased since the end of the apostolic age and the completion of the New Testament. Divine revelation was given during the foundational work of the apostles and prophets (Eph. 2:20). When these men passed away, their gifts did as well. Logically, tongues ceased at this point as well, since tongues are associated with these two gifts in verse 8. All three gifts are specifically mentioned together, and the same assertion is made for all three. It would disrupt the cohesion of the passage to give one of the gifts a different ceasing point than the other two.

History bears record to the cessation of tongues as well. It wasn't until the end of the nineteenth century that somebody claimed to speak in tongues, about eighteen hundred years after the apostles. Although there were some minor heretical groups that spoke in tongues, tongues are not a legitimate part of post-apostolic church history. Historically, they had ceased.

Claim #2: Tongues-speaking is evidence of salvation or spirituality

The second claim is a dangerous teaching that has ensnared many. To claim that tongues-speaking is evidence of salvation is clearly unbiblical. The Bible never uses the ability to speak in tongues as an indication of salvation or of spirituality. There are many accounts of salvation in Acts where tongue-speaking does not happen. The true proof of salvation is a person's victory over sin or increased knowledge of God. It is at this point that we can begin to see the true flaw of modern claims to tongues: they knowingly elevate experience over the Word of God. Instead of bringing their practices and beliefs into conformity with God's Word, they manipulate God's Word to fit their practices.

Claim #3: Tongues are ecstatic speech

Again, this assertion contradicts what the Bible teaches con-cerning tongues. Acts 2 shows that tongues were foreign lan-guages. The Jewish men did not hear the disciples speaking in gibberish and then wonder what they said. According to verse 6, "every man heard them speak in his own language." The Greek word for *language* in this verse is *dialectos*. (You can see that we get our word *dialect* from this root.) It signifies a language group; though *dialectos* could also mean a dialect within a language, it more often refers to a language itself, such as German or Spanish. In this passage, the Jewish hearers identified seventeen different groups that were hearing the gospel in their own language (2:9-11). The grammar and context of the passage is clear: tongues were known foreign languages.

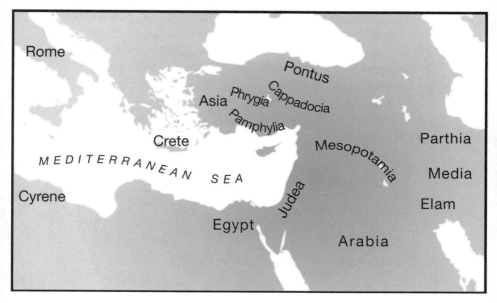

Claim #4: An unlimited number of speakers are permitted in a service

The last assertion, or really practice, of modern groups also reveals the elevation of experience over God's Word. More than three tongues-speakers and more than one at a time are common occurrences at Charismatic services. In addition, women are allowed to speak with the same authority as men. All three of these practices demonstrate disobedience to the Word of God (I Cor. 14). Even if we assume for the sake of argument that the gift of tongues is still active today, there are very few groups (if any) that practice this gift within the boundaries of biblical revelation. It may be also added that the chaotic spirit of modern "tongues" services is antithetical to the nature of our God. God is not the author of confusion; He is the author of order (I Cor. 14:33). Though there are some true Christians within the Charismatic movement, many have been deceived into replacing the truth with error.

The Charismatics have wrongly elevated the significance of tongues. In short, they have replaced the desire for truth with the desire for supernatural experience. In their effort to defend their movement, they have taken an attitude toward sign gifts different from that of the apostles. They have also disregarded the greater necessity of exercising love with spiritual gifts. In I Corinthians 13, Paul gives the greatest definition of love ever found. And though tongues and prophecy have ceased, love will continue forever. It behooves us, therefore, to examine, not only what our gifts are but whether we are practicing the "more excellent way" of love.

The Necessity of Love in the Exercise of Gifts

"I would love to go for a walk with you."

"I don't know about hot dogs, but I sure do love pizza."

"I love you, Karina. Will you marry me?"

"He sold out his family for the love of money."

"I love you too, Dad."

"I love you guys. You are some of my best friends."

"Love is a choice."

"Do you remember when we first fell in love? I think it was the summer of '54."

"Thou shalt love the Lord your God with all your heart."

"If you see Johnny, send him my love."

Talk about a multi-meaning word! Depending on how you use the word *love,* you could mean a variety of things. Each example above uses the word with a different connotation. You could say that the word communicates different levels of love in different contexts. Your love for your pet is probably not as strong as your love for your best friend, which is not as strong as your love for your parents, which is not as strong as your love will be for your spouse, which should never be as strong as your love for God. All of these manifest varying degrees of love. It's no wonder, then, that confusion sometimes results when someone speaks of biblical love.

Because our society has perverted the concept of love, we need to spend time meditating on what the Bible says about true love. Whereas the Colossian church modeled biblical love (Col. 1:8), the Corinthian church desperately needed it. It is no wonder then that we find the longest passage on love in I Corinthians 13. However, we cannot remove this chapter from its context. Although the chapter can rightly be applied to many relationships, its contextual application is to the exercise of spiritual gifts within the church. So how does Paul define love?

He doesn't. Instead, he states what love does. First Corinthians 13:4-7 is a list of fifteen specific actions that love performs on behalf of other believers. That should immediately dispel the notion that love is primarily a feeling or an emotion. Although true love will carry emotion with it sometimes, feeling is not a necessary ingredient of love, nor is it the basis. Therefore, biblical love is not a feeling: it's an action. As we examine each of these actions, we need to humbly inspect our own hearts to see if we truly love other members of Christ's church. We need to examine closely what love does.

Biblical love is not a feeling; it's an action.

Charity suffereth long,
And is kind;
Charity envieth not;
Charity vaunteth not itself,
Is not puffed up,

Doth not behave itself unseemly,
Seeketh not her own,
Is not easily provoked,
Thinketh no evil;

Rejoiceth not in iniquity,
But rejoiceth in the truth;

Beareth all things,
Believeth all things,
Hopeth all things,
Endureth all things.

The Essentials of Love

The first phrase of verse 4 uses the words *suffereth long* to describe love. This verb is very picturesque. It has to do with restraining anger. The Greek word is actually a compound of two words, *long* and *wrath.* In other words, a person who suffers long takes a long time to get angry. You can't "tick him off" easily or make him explode quickly. He is not short-tempered. That means if you truly love other Christians, you will put up with them. Irritation is not an option—no matter how badly the person may offend you or "rub you the wrong way." Biblical love suffers long.

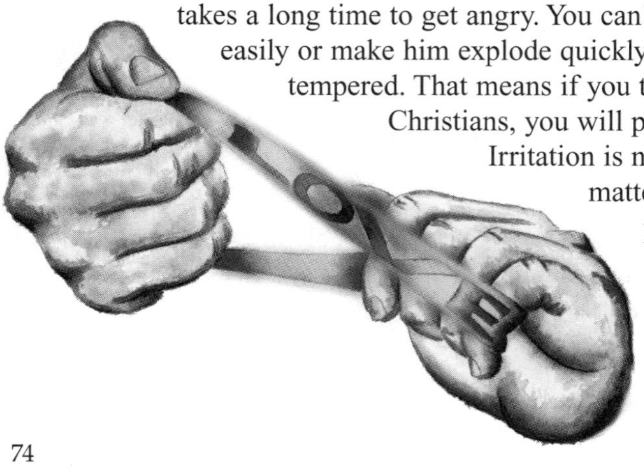

The second statement in verse 4 could be more literally translated "graces," since the underlying Greek behind *is kind* is actually a verb. I point that out in order to reaffirm that love is an action. Whereas *suffering long* is a restraining action, *is kind* is a giving action. It refers to benevolent actions, such as bringing a meal to a widow who is sick, mowing the lawn for someone else in the neighborhood, making a card to encourage another believer, or just plain smiling to brighten somebody's day. The verb is rich in meaning and plenteous in examples. Essentially, though, it describes somebody who is always seeking to be gracious to another person, whether that means giving time, money, or effort. This person never thinks about how long it will take, how much it will cost, or how much it will require. He is more interested in acting kindly. Does this describe you?

The Denials of Love

The next set of verbs deals with denials. A person who loves others denies and restrains himself. The first three denials concern pride: "Charity envieth not; charity vaunteth not itself, is not puffed up." The verb *envieth* carries strong emotion. It conveys the emotions of jealousy and wrath. A person who envies is singularly concerned with self—self-ambition, self-advancement, and self-glory. If you get in the way of his advancement or if you advance ahead of him, he is jealous of you and seethes with contempt. A person who loves, however, denies these emotions. He doesn't vaunt himself and is not puffed up. These self-denials have been forgotten in the world of sports. Egos and boastful words are almost essential ingredients for stardom. The entertainment industry even produces commercials of players bragging about themselves. Bragging and being puffed up, though, isn't a part of love. It's part of Satan's insidious plan to destroy and break down the church. If members of the church are envious of one another and puffed up, edification is not happening. Pride hinders edification; love accelerates it. If you are guilty of always seeking the limelight and wanting people to notice you, you are guilty of a heinous sin that God hates. You are also guilty of a sin that directly hinders the edification of Christ's body.

The next denial concerns maturity: "[Love] does not behave itself unseemly" (v. 5). This verb eradicates the notion that being boisterous or acting foolishly is part of being a teen. Christ demands that even teenagers act in a way that is becoming, or fitting of a person who loves. That means when you have the temptation to ridicule someone or tease to the point that someone's feelings are hurt, you must resist the urge. Being rude is unloving. Loving means being well-mannered.

The final denial concerns seeking your own glory: "[Love] seeketh not her own" (v. 5). Love does not put self above others. The exact opposite is true. Love seeks the success of others. It exerts effort in order that another member of the body be edified. It does not sit back in a pew and wait to be served by others. If all the members of the church would follow this admonition, there would be much less strife and division.

The five denials of love could be summarized in one word—humility. A loving person is a humble person. He doesn't push himself above others, he doesn't want recognition from men, and he doesn't try to get the glory. He genuinely wants to edify others and to glorify God. It is no wonder that Christ said the greatest two commandments are loving God and loving your neighbor (Matt. 22:37-40). On these two commandments hang all the other commandments.

The Determinations of Love

The next set of actions that love exercises is specific determinations. They are deep-seated convictions that have been resolved ahead of time. The first determination of love is a resolve not to be provoked. You must refuse to allow somebody to stir you to anger. When a guy on the opposing basketball team pushes you in the back, you have already determined that you will not retaliate or blow up. Your testimony before the Lord is too important to allow others to provoke you. Your circumstances should not determine your level of love.

The second determination of love is a refusal to think evil of another person. The verb is actually an accounting term. It means "to log away" or "to keep record." It's similar to keeping a checkbook. The verse is actually stating that love does not keep a record of a person's sins. In other words, you cannot keep a log of all the things people have done to harm you. If God blesses you with a marriage and children, you will need to exercise this love many times. So many marriages suffer because of a failure to think no evil.

The last determination of love involves truth and error: "[Love] rejoiceth not in iniquity, but rejoiceth in the truth." A Spirit-empowered person loves veracity. He rejoices to learn truth from God's Word, and he hates the transgression of it. A person demonstrates this love as a reflection of God's character. As you draw near to God, you will learn to love what He loves and hate what He hates. Do you realize that enjoyment of gossip is a violation of this determination? If you truly love others, you will not delight to hear about their problems or failures. Instead, you should desire to hear things that are pure and right; you should deny "access" to your ears to those things that are iniquitous in nature. Do you enjoy portrayals of violence? This too is a violation of this determination. You are told not to rejoice in iniquity—that includes movies or TV shows that glorify shooting, killing, and other acts of sin. There is nothing wholesome or pure about a "bloody fight." God hates the soul that loves violence (Ps. 11:5).

The Immeasurability of Love

Love has no bounds; it is limitless. The last four verbs emphasize this truth: "Beareth all things, believeth all things, hopeth all things, endureth all things." The repetition of *all things* extends love to immeasurable distances. Once again, we will look at each verb to gain a better understanding of love's activity.

Roof over it! That's the meaning of the first verb, which is actually taken from the noun form for "roof." Although we generally think about bearing as enduring, to bear all things means to cover over all things. Love doesn't throw past sins back in somebody's face. It doesn't point out a person's flaws or recall a person's failure. If forgiveness has been granted, love just "roofs" over it. It's a wonderful picture of Christian love, the same picture that Peter talks about: "And above all things have fervent charity among yourselves: for charity shall cover the multitude of sins" (I Pet. 4:8). As in all aspects of love, Christ modeled this forgiveness perfectly. The greatest picture of "roofing love" is our own salvation: Christ covered our sins with His own blood. If Christ was willing to roof over our sins, shouldn't you be willing to forgive others?

> *The greatest picture of "roofing love" is our own salvation: Christ covered our sins with His own blood.*

The second immeasurable activity of love is that it "believeth all things." This statement is not advocating a blind naiveté, but it is asserting that you should not search for hidden motives or always assume evil. Love values a person and considers him or her to be worthy of trust. It takes a person at his word. Love says, "I trust you." A good biblical example of this is Barnabas and Paul. When Paul was first converted, many of the disciples thought he was faking it so that he could learn where they were hiding. But Barnabas exercised love by believing Paul's testimony and taking him to the disciples.

The third verb, *hope,* ties in well with believing. *Hope* means "to expect the best." A hopeful person eagerly expects the best of somebody, rather than assuming the worst. To put it another way, *hoping all things* means giving others the benefit of the doubt. When a person arrives late to a meeting, love assumes that the

Lessons in Roofing

Think About It!

Read the following conversation between Jesus and Peter. What was Jesus' explicit roofing lesson for Peter?

"Then came Peter to him, and said, Lord, how oft shall my brother sin against me, and I forgive him? till seven times?

Jesus saith unto him, I say not unto thee, Until seven times: but, Until seventy times seven. Therefore is the kingdom of heaven likened unto a certain king, which would take account of his servants. And when he had begun to reckon, one was brought unto him, which owed him ten thousand talents. But forasmuch as he had not to pay, his lord commanded him to be sold, and his wife, and children, and all that he had, and payment to be made. The servant therefore fell down, and worshipped him, saying, Lord, have patience with me, and I will pay thee all. Then the lord of that servant was moved with compassion, and loosed him, and forgave him the debt. But the same servant went out, and found one of his fellowservants, which owed him an hundred pence: And he laid hands on him, and took him by the throat, saying, Pay me that thou owest. And his fellowservant fell down at his feet, and besought him, saying, Have patience with me, and I will pay thee all. And he would not: but went and cast him into prison, till he should pay the debt. So when his fellowservants saw what was done, they were very sorry, and came and told unto their lord all that was done. Then his lord, after that he had called him, said unto him, O thou wicked servant, I forgave thee all that debt, because thou desiredst me: Shouldest not thou also have had compassion on thy fellowservant, even as I had pity on thee? And his lord was wroth, and delivered him to the tormentors, till he should pay all that was due unto him. So likewise shall my heavenly Father do also unto you, if ye from your hearts forgive not every one his brother their trespasses (Matt. 18:21-35).

person was honestly delayed; it doesn't think that the person was just lazy. Your parents have probably demonstrated this type of hope numerous times with you. They always hope for the best from you. They "believe" in you. You can almost see your mom pulling out her pictures from her purse: "And this is Stephen. He's so handsome. (*Sigh*) He'll make a fine man some day." That's the type of hope that we must exhibit within the body of Christ. You have to expect that the person will succeed. Again, Barnabas exemplifies this hope. Do you remember John Mark? For whatever reasons, he deserted Paul and Barnabas on their first missionary journey. When it came time for the second missionary trip, Paul was unwilling to take John Mark. But Barnabas hoped all things. He expected that John Mark would stay this time and be a successful missionary. Though Paul disagreed at the time, he later agreed. He even described John Mark as being "profitable . . . for the ministry" (II Tim. 4:11). What about you? Do you "hope all things" for your parents? your siblings? your classmates?

The final action of love that Paul lists as immeasurable is endurance. Love endures all things. It keeps going under all types of pressure and circumstances. True love is resilient, reliable, and steadfast. In an age of decayed morals and destroyed marriages, Christians need to show that true love persists. It doesn't quit when money gets tight, circumstances go sour, or people fail. If a person truly loves another person, he will endure all things.

Endurance is an absolute necessity for love—whether in the church, in the home, or at the office. Though a person may exercise the first fourteen verbs that exemplify love, if he doesn't endure, then he has failed. True love endures. "Love never fails."

Conclusion: So What Gift Do I Have?

You have probably asked that question a few times already as you have been reading, and rightly so. If the Bible teaches that every believer has a spiritual gift, you should want to know how the Spirit has specially enabled you to edify other members of the church. There is great satisfaction and joy knowing that you are directly fulfilling God's will by using your gift. So how do you find your gift? Well, it's not by doing close introspection on your personality, examining what you like or don't like. It is probably not found by taking 100-question exams that claim to tell you your spiritual gift. The answer is actually quite simple—serve! Finding your spiritual gift comes by engaging yourself in Christian service.

As you serve, observe how Christians respond to what you are doing or saying. That doesn't mean that you are trying to please men, but it does mean that you are seeking to build up the body of Christ. Other mature members of the body will notice and comment on your edification. It makes sense that if your gift is for the edifying of the body, then others will perceive your ministry to them. Think of your own experience as a Christian. Have you ever been edified by somebody who had the gift of teaching? How did you recognize it? You probably didn't think to yourself, *This person is exercising the gift of teaching.* But you probably knew that you were being ministered to spiritually. Likewise, you will discover your spiritual gift(s) as you serve in different capacities.

It is interesting to note that of the four passages that list different sets of spiritual gifts, no two lists are exactly the same. Some gifts are in only one passage;

some gifts are in two or three passages. Because of this, it is safe to conclude that the Spirit never intended to list exhaustively all of the gifts. Therefore, your gift may not necessarily be listed. I can think of one great example—music. No passage lists music as a spiritual gift, but no church service would be complete without it. Regardless of what your particular gift may be, the important thing is to exercise it in love. The desire to know your spiritual gift is a great thing, but the desire to love is the more excellent way (I Cor. 12:31).

Review Questions

Matching

Answers may be used more than once.

A. Acts 2   F. I Cor. 13
B. Acts 10   G. I Cor. 14
C. Acts 19   H. Eph. 4
D. Rom. 12   I. I Pet. 4
E. I Cor. 12

_____1. Regulations for tongues-speaking

_____2. Jews speak in tongues.

_____3. Gentiles speak in tongues.

_____4. Tongues will cease.

_____5. Emphasis on the source of gifts

_____6. Two-category division of gifts

_____7. Christ gives gifted men for edification.

_____8. Having a gift is being a steward of grace.

_____9. Gifts should enhance harmony.

_____10. Quotation of Isaiah 28:11

_____11. Love is the more excellent way.

_____12. John's disciples speak in tongues.

_____13. Tongues are known foreign languages.

_____14. Sacrifice is unprofitable without love.

_____15. Gifts are for the "work of the ministry."

_____16. Exhortation "not to think too highly" of self

17. How do we know that tongues are not signs for believers?

18. Of the fifteen descriptions of love in I Corinthians 13, in what areas do you need to change the most?

19. Samantha complains that she doesn't participate in church activities because she doesn't know what her gift is. What biblical counsel could you give to her?

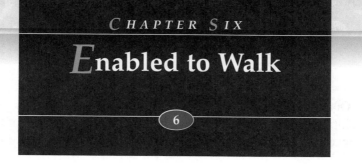

CHAPTER SIX

*E*nabled to Walk

6

"C'mon. C'mon, Elias. Walk to Uncle Damon." It wasn't too long ago that I was trying to get my nephew Elias to take his first steps. I had seen my sister and brother-in-law give the same encouragement several times before. My nephew would stand, shake a little bit, pretend to take a step, and then collapse to a seated position. Within a few weeks, however, he was walking around with ease. His legs were strong enough, and he had learned the basic procedure of putting one foot in front of the other. Although the Bible uses many descriptions for our spiritual progress, it most often uses the analogy of walking. In fact, almost every book of the Bible uses the analogy.

Walking is a facet of life that is familiar to all of us. Unfortunately, spiritual walking is not as familiar. But just as learning to walk physically requires knowledge and strength, spiritual walking requires wisdom and power. The Spirit provides these for the believer at salvation. However, the enjoyment of His wisdom and power grows with experience. You cannot have a wise and powerful walk apart from submitting to the Spirit. In this chapter, we will explore exactly what it means to walk in the Spirit and to enjoy His gracious provisions.

1999-2002 © www.arttoday.com

Wisdom to Walk—The Spirit's Anointing

One of the works of the Spirit that is overlooked often is anointing. Before we discuss how anointing affects the life of the believer, we need to define the term. What is the anointing of the Spirit?

Anointing Defined

There are two direct references in Scripture to the Spirit's anointing. The first reference is II Corinthians 1:21-22, where Paul refers to the anointing that he and the Corinthian Christians received from God. The second reference, in I John 2:20-27, states that the anointing is from the Holy One and that the anointing abides in believers. Verse 27 even states that the "anointing teaches you." By putting all of these verses together, we can for-

mulate a definition. The anointing of the Spirit is *the Spirit's rendering the believer capable of understanding truth.* At salvation the Spirit enables the person to comprehend God's Word. He gives him spiritual vision. We can safely conclude that anointing is an instantaneous action performed at salvation, because it is referred to in both passages as a past action for all believers.

Before a person is regenerated and indwelled by the Spirit, he is unable to perceive the things of God. I Corinthians 2:9-14 explains,

"But as it is written, Eye hath not seen, nor ear heard, neither have entered into the heart of man, the things which God hath prepared for them that love him. But God hath revealed them unto us by his Spirit: for the Spirit searcheth all things, yea, the deep things of God. For what man knoweth the things of a man, save the spirit of man which is in him? even so the things of God knoweth no man, but the Spirit of God. Now we have received, not the spirit of the world, but the Spirit which is of God; that we might know the things that are freely given to us of God. Which things also we speak, not in the words which man's wisdom teacheth, but which the Holy Ghost teacheth; comparing spiritual things with spiritual. But the natural man receiveth not the things of the Spirit of God: for they are foolishness unto him: neither can he know them, because they are spiritually discerned."

These verses clarify exactly what the Spirit is doing now in the hearts of believers. He is making known the mind of God. How does the Spirit reveal God's mind?

Effects of Anointing

The first effect of the Spirit's anointing is illumination. When we seek to know the Spirit's mind on something, we are really seeking to know what He has revealed in Scripture. We are praying that He would guide us to the right passage or that He would show us which passages to put together. Because the Spirit is our anointing, we can be sure that He will lead us into truth. The anointing work of the Spirit guarantees that we will be able to grasp God's Word. It doesn't guarantee, however, that we will be able to grasp everything at once. As we daily rely upon the Spirit to teach us from the Word, we will increase in our knowledge of God and our ability to apply that knowledge. That increasing is illumination. Though the act of anointing occurs once for all at

When we seek the Spirit's mind, we are really seeking to know what He has revealed in Scripture.

salvation, its benefits and effects can be continuously enjoyed if the Christian will seek the Spirit's illumination. Many Christians wander without direction because they are not availing themselves of the illumination of the Spirit's anointing. Listen to what one author writes:

"To Christians who are spiritual, i.e., filled with the Spirit, it is possible for the Spirit to reveal the deep things of God. In the extended revelation of this truth in I Corinthians 2:9–3:2, it is made clear that the deeper things of spiritual truth can be understood only by those who are spiritually qualified to be taught by the Spirit. The natural man is unable to understand even the simple truths understood by those who are Spirit-taught. The appalling ignorance of many Christians concerning the things of the Word of God is directly traceable to their carnality and failure in seeking the blessings of a life filled with the Spirit."[1]

The second benefit of the Spirit's anointing is guidance. The Spirit promises to guide believers into truth and help them make the right decisions. The Bible records that the Spirit would aid the disciples in what to say when they were under persecution (Matt. 10:20; Mark 13:11; Luke 12:12). The Spirit led Philip to the desert and other places to witness (Acts 8:29, 39). The Spirit informed Paul about his future bonds and afflictions and guided him to Jerusalem (Acts 19:21; 20:22; 21:4). The Spirit also sent out Paul and Barnabas as missionaries (Acts 13:4) and gave instruction concerning church rules (Acts 15:28) and church gov-

ernment (Acts 20:28). According to Jude 20, we are to pray in the Spirit, which means that our prayers are to be guided by His will. In the Old Testament, David prayed for the Spirit's leading (Ps. 143:10), and the Spirit guided Israel to rest (Isa. 63:14), though they rebelled at times against His guidance (Ps. 106:33; Acts 7:51).

Although this may seem puzzling at first, the Spirit may even lead a person to be tempted. The

Spirit led Christ to be tempted by Satan, empowered Him to over-come, and ministered to Him after the temptation (Matt. 4:1; Mark 1:12; Luke 4:1). That means that you can be in the center of God's will and full of the Spirit and still undergo temptation. Being tempted is not a sin; yielding to temptation is. The safest place to be during temptation is yielded to the Spirit's leading. When we are guided by the Spirit, we can be assured of His presence and power. We can praise Him that He will never lead us into a temptation that we cannot handle.

Strength to Walk—The Spirit's Empowerment

The Bible gives much information about the Spirit's empowerment of the believer. The Old Testament contains several examples of believers who were empowered; the most noteworthy were the judges. The Spirit empowered Othniel (Judg. 3:10), Gideon (6:34), Jephthah (11:29), and Samson (13:25; 14:6, 19; 15:14). We also read that the Spirit empowered David (I Sam. 16:13), Micah (Mic. 3:8), and others. Zechariah records that nothing can be accomplished for the Lord apart from the Spirit (4:6). New Testament examples include John the Baptist and his parents, who were all said to be full of the Spirit (Luke 1:15, 41, 67). We know, of course, that the Anointed One was empowered by the Spirit. That characteristic of His life was prophesied several times by Isaiah (42:1; 48:16; 59:21; 61:1) and recorded by the Gospel writers (Matt. 12:18, 28; Luke 4:18; 10:21; John 3:34). The Spirit's descent at Christ's baptism signified that the Spirit was on the Messiah (Luke 3:22; John 1:32).

Pentecost began an age characterized by an outpouring of the Spirit upon the lives of every saved person. Christ promised this universal empowerment during His earthly ministry and resurrection appearances (Luke 11:13). In John 7:38-39, Christ had promised that those who would believe in Him would have rivers of water flowing from their innermost being. The imagery signifies living power that is unstoppable in its force. Christians have the omnipotent Holy Spirit dwelling within them. Christ also promised the Spirit's power in Acts 1:8. Peter identifies the fulfillment of this prophecy in Acts 2:17, 18, and 33, affirming that Christ poured out the Spirit on all believers.

Christians have the omnipotent Holy Spirit dwelling within them

Luke records instances of the Spirit's empowerment in numerous other places in Acts. The 120 were empowered to speak in tongues in Acts 2:4. Peter was filled with the Holy Spirit in 4:8, and in 4:31 the disciples received power to preach the gospel after praying. Acts 6:3 requires that deacons be full of the Spirit. Stephen is said to be Spirit-filled three times (6:5, 10; 7:55). In

Acts 9:17, Ananias was sent so that Paul would receive his sight and so that he would be filled with the Holy Spirit. Acts 11:24 records that Barnabas was full of faith and the Holy Ghost. Luke later writes that the disciples were filled with the Holy Spirit (Acts 13:9, 52). The Bible is emphasizing that the disciples were supernaturally empowered to accomplish the work of God. They were not superhumans who could not sin. They were redeemed sinners who walked in the power of the Spirit. This is the same power that Paul prays we would know and display (Eph. 3:16). If we can learn anything from their examples, it is the following two lessons.

1. **Empowerment is something that can be prayed for.** Acts 4:24-30 records the disciples' prayer after being persecuted. They asked for boldness to give out the gospel of Christ, and their prayer was answered. They realized their own weakness and inability to fulfill God's will, but they also realized that through God's Spirit they could do anything. As they relied on the Spirit to work through them, He empowered them to preach. Verse 31 states that the Spirit *filled* them. That terminology brings up the second point.

2. **Empowerment depends on filling.** In the New Testament, the Bible speaks about a person being filled with the Spirit or being full of the Spirit. These words describe a person who is yielded to the Spirit. Being filled with the Spirit means *being submitted to His influence.* We know that this definition is correct from Ephesians 5:18. In this verse, Paul compares being filled with the Spirit to being drunk with wine. When someone is drunk with wine, they are under the influence of the alcohol. They no longer think reasonably or rationally because the intoxicating chemicals in the alcohol are controlling them. The point of similarity between being drunk and being filled with the Spirit is the controlling influence. Whereas Paul commands us not to be under the controlling influence of wine, he does command us to be under the controlling influence of the Spirit. When we submit to the Spirit, He empowers us and we are said to be full of the Spirit. In other words, we are empowered because we are submitted.

Taylor and His Half Crown

We often think of missionaries as super-Christians, men and women who reach an elite level of spirituality. After all, we have heard about their heroic achievements for Christ, their faith that seemingly moved mountains, and the countless souls that were saved under their ministries. But missionaries struggle too. They also have to yield to the Spirit's leading before they can accomplish God's will. J. Hudson Taylor, the great missionary to China, was no exception. Here are his own words about his fierce struggle concerning money.

My kind employer, always busy, wished me to remind him whenever my salary became due. This I determined not to do directly but to ask that God would bring the fact to his recollection and thus encourage me by answering prayer. At one time as the day drew near for the payment of a quarter's salary, I was as usual much in prayer about it. The time arrived, but Dr. Hardey made no allusion to the matter. I continued praying. Days passed on, and he did not remember, until at length, on settling up weekly accounts one Saturday night, I found myself possessed of only one remaining coin, a half crown piece. Still, I had hitherto known no lack, and I continued praying.

That Sunday was a very happy one. As usual my heart was full and brimming over the blessing. After attending divine service in the morning, my afternoons and evenings were taken up with gospel work in the various lodging houses I was accustomed to visit in the lowest part of the town. At such times it almost seemed to me as if heaven were begun below, and that all that could be looked for was an enlargement of one's capacity for joy, not a truer filling than I possessed.

After concluding my last service about ten o'clock that night, a poor man asked me to go and pray with his wife, saying that she was dying. I readily agreed, and on the way to his house asked him why he had not sent for the priest, as his accent told me he was an Irishman. He had done so, he said, but the priest refused to come without a payment of eighteen pence which the man did not possess, as the family was starving. Immediately it occurred to my mind that all the money I had in the world was the solitary half crown, and that it was in one coin; moreover, that while the basin of water gruel I usually took for supper was awaiting me, and there was sufficient in the house for breakfast in the morning, I certainly had nothing for dinner on the coming day.

"Ah," thought I, "if only I had two shillings and a sixpence instead of this half crown, how gladly would I give these poor people a shilling!" But to part with the half crown was far from my thoughts. I little dreamed that the truth of the matter simply was that I could trust God plus one and sixpence but was not prepared to trust Him only, without any money at all in my pocket.

My conductor led me into a court, down which I followed him. . . . Up a miserable flight of stairs into a wretched room he led me, and oh, what a sight there presented itself! Four or five children stood about, their sunken cheeks and temples all telling unmistakably the story of slow starvation, and lying on a wretched pallet was a poor, exhausted mother, with a tiny infant thirty-six hours old, moaning rather than crying at her side, for it too seemed spent and failing.

"Ah!" thought I, "if I had two shillings and a sixpence, instead of a half crown, how gladly should they have one and sixpence of it." But still a wretched unbelief prevented me from obeying the impulse to relieve their distress at the cost of all I possessed.

"You asked me to come and pray with your wife," I said to the man, "let us pray." And I knelt down.

But no sooner had I opened my lips with "Our Father who art in heaven," than the conscience said within, "Dare you mock God? Dare you kneel down and call Him Father with that half crown in your pocket?"

I arose from my knees in great distress of mind. The poor father turned to me and said, "You see what a terrible state we are in, sir. IF you can help us, for God's sake do!"

At that moment the word flashed into my mind, "Give to him that asketh [of] thee" (Matt. 5:42). And in the word of a King there is power. I put my hand into my pocket, and slowly drawing out the half crown, gave it to the man, telling him that it might seem a small matter for me to relieve them, seeing that I was comparatively well off, but that in parting with that coin I was giving him my all; what I had been trying to tell them was indeed true—God really was a FA-THER and might be trusted. The joy all came back in full flood tide to my heart. I could say anything and feel it then, and the hindrance to blessing was gone—gone, I trust, forever.

Not only was the poor woman's life saved, but my life, as I fully realized, had been saved too. It might have been a wreck—would have been probably, as a Christian life—had not grace at that time conquered and the striving of God's Spirit been obeyed.[2]

So when the Bible speaks of men and women who were full of the Spirit, it is speaking of people who were submitted to the Holy Spirit and were being empowered to do His will. It is also giving us examples to follow. The terms *Spirit-controlled* and *Spirit-empowered* should characterize every Christian's life. If you want the power of the Spirit in your life, you must submit to Him. You do not need more of the Spirit; the Spirit needs more of you. Too many people are deceived into thinking that they need to have another experience with the Spirit, when what they really need is to submit to what He has already shown them. The Bible is clear to those who are genuinely seeking. The key to empowerment is being filled with the Spirit.

A Wise and Powerful Walk

So far in this chapter we've established that the Spirit's anointing and empowerment *equip* the believer to walk before the Lord and that the *experience* of these works depends on his submission to the Spirit. (Remember, being submitted to the Spirit means being filled with the Spirit.) We have not discussed, however, some of the changes that this submission produces. For instance, one of these characteristics is a changed mindset. Romans 8:5-6 states, "For they that are after the flesh do mind the things of the flesh; but they that are after the Spirit the things of the Spirit. For to be carnally minded is death; but to be spiritually minded is life and peace." A believer who is walking after the Spirit minds the things of the Spirit. He is actively choosing to think about the Spirit's teaching. If you are a Spirit-filled believer, you will be concerned about what the Spirit

CHRISTLIKENESS

convicts   gifts
indwells   regenerates
baptizes   calls
fills
empowers   illumines

thinks about the places you go, the friends you enjoy, and the decisions you make. Your mind should not ask, "Do I like this music?" but rather, "Does this music please the Spirit?" or "Will this music lead me to be more Spirit-filled, or will it make me more carnally-minded?"

Having the Spirit's mind will shape how you act. A spiritual mind leads to a spiritual life. The opposite is also true. A carnal mind leads to a carnal life. If your desire is to grow in your walk with God, you must submit to the Spirit's control. As you do, He will illumine you and empower you to walk with a spiritual mindset. Not to submit is to be at enmity with God, a possible sign that you may never have been regenerated. Paul gives both a warning and a blessing concerning this matter. "For if ye live after the flesh, ye shall die; but if ye through the Spirit do mortify the deeds of the body, ye shall live. For as many as are led by the Spirit of God, they are the sons of God" (Rom. 8:13-14). True believers are led by God's Spirit. It is a sign of their regeneration.

A spiritual mind leads to a spiritual life.

Other Bible passages teach that the Spirit's all-encompassing purpose for the believer is Christlikeness. He convicts, calls, regenerates, indwells, baptizes, bestows gifts, fills, illumines, and empowers the believer for the one great purpose of making the believer more like Christ. He is constantly sanctifying us to be more like the Savior. Therefore, we must yield as clay to the Spirit's control so that He can mold us into the image of Christ. That truth is clearly taught in II Corinthians 3:18: "But we all, with open face beholding as in a glass the glory of the Lord, are changed into the same image from glory to glory, even as by the Spirit of the Lord." As we peer into the Word of God (the glass) and see the Lord, the Spirit changes us into that image. The Scripture even says that the indwelling Spirit is jealous concerning this sanctification (James 4:5). We, in turn, should be jealous to be sanctified by the Spirit.

Mortification: A Fight to the Death

The Bible uses some pretty powerful words to describe our struggle against sin. In Romans 8:13 and Colossians 3:5, Paul tells us to mortify the deeds and desires of the flesh. In other words, kill sin! Sniff it out, hunt it down, and strike it dead. Though murder of humans is not biblically sanctioned, murder of sin is divinely intended.

As you read the words of John Owen concerning mortification, pray that the Spirit would empower you to put to death the deeds of the flesh. Owen masterfully explains this key aspect to sanctification.

THE DUTY OF MORTIFICATION

The duty of mortification is to take sides with grace against sin. This means cherishing and strengthening the ruling principle of holiness implanted in us by the Holy Spirit. It means letting grace freely work in us all duties, both internal and external. In this way the activities of the flesh are defeated. It means applying the appropriate grace, with all its power and activity, against that particular sin which desires to be fulfilled. Just as there are particular sins which desire to be fulfilled, so there is a particular grace to oppose each sin. When mortifying a particular sin, that particular grace designed to oppose that particular sin must be brought into play. It is in this right application of the appropriate grace to the particular sin that the secret of mortification lies. This duty of weakening sin by the strengthening of grace in order to oppose sin is called mortification, or putting to death; first, because it is the actual putting to death of indwelling sin, and second, because it is a violent duty. All other duties may be performed in an easier and gentler manner, yet in this duty we are to wrestle, to fight and to kill. Thirdly, it is called mortification because the whole purpose of this duty is the final and utter destruction of indwelling sin.

HOW TO MORTIFY SIN

Determine that you will, every day and in every duty, abolish and destroy this ruling principle of sin. It will not die unless it is gradually and constantly weakened. Spare it, and it heals its wounds and recovers its strength. Negligence allows sin to regain such power that we may never recover our former state as long as we live.

We are continually to watch out for the rising up of the ruling principle of sin and immediately subdue it. This is to be done in all that we are and do. We are to be watchful in our behaviour to others, watchful when we are alone, watchful when in trouble or joy. We are to be particularly watchful in the use of our pleasure times and in temptations.

Determine that you will no longer serve sin (Rom. 6:6). See it as the worst service of which a rational creature is capable. If you serve sin it will bring you to a dreadful end. Determine that though sin remains in you, yet you will not serve it. Remember, if the 'old man' is not crucified with Christ, you are still a servant of sin, whatever you might think of yourself.

Realise that it is no easy task to mortify sin. Sin is a powerful and dreadful enemy. There is no living thing that will not do everything in its power to save its life. So sin also will fight to save its life. If sin is not diligently hunted down and dealt with by holy violence, it will escape all our attempts at killing it. It is a great mistake to think that we can at any time rest from this duty. The ruling principle of sin to be slain is in us, and so has hold of all our faculties. Sin cannot be killed without a sense of pain and trouble. So Christ compared it to 'cutting off the right hand' and 'plucking out the right eye'. The battle is not against any particular lust but against all sinful lusts which war against the soul.

Although mortification is our duty, it is by the grace and strength of the Holy Spirit that we are enabled to do it. That the duty of mortification is the Holy Spirit's work is asserted by Paul (Rom. 8:13). We are to mortify the deeds of the flesh. But we are able to do this only by the Holy Spirit. We cannot do it by our own power and ability.[3]

These words by Owen give us the sobering reality that mortification is both our duty and the Spirit's duty. However, we cannot expect the Spirit to enable us to put off sin and put on righteousness if we are not obeying Him. If we are failing to read His Word, to pray according to His will, and to attend His house of worship, we will not overcome sin in our lives. Only by following His voice can we know victory. Sanctification is His work (Rom. 15:16; I Cor. 6:11; II Cor. 3:3). What about you? Are you yielding to His sanctifying work?

Yielding to the Spirit, however, is not always easy, since our adversary, the Devil, seeks to gain control over our lives. Our flesh also strives against the Spirit and seeks to control our lives (Gal. 5:17). But if we will use the Sword of the Spirit, we can ward off Satan (Eph. 6:17), and if we yield to the Spirit we will not give in to the lusts of the flesh (Gal. 5:16). Instead, we will be led by the Spirit to produce Christlike attributes (Gal. 5:18-25). The lists given in Galatians 5:18-25 contrast the flesh and the Spirit. On one hand you have the fruit of Satan-like qualities produced by the flesh; on the other hand, you have the Christlike qualities produced by the Spirit. Paul sums up this discussion of opposing fruits in verse 25. "If we live in the Spirit, let us also walk in the Spirit." Regeneration is by the Spirit through faith; sanctification is by the Spirit through faith. The choice is rather simple; the way is rather rough. But if you submit to the Spirit, He will empower you to fight against the flesh. Rejecting sanctification is the same as rejecting God who gives you the Holy Spirit (I Thess. 4:8).

Conclusion

By enlightening you and strengthening you, the Spirit is seeking to produce spiritual fruit in your life. He is giving you the knowledge to walk by God's Word and the strength to walk by His power. Yet a Spirit-led walk can be maintained only as you submit to His leadership. So how are you walking? Are your steps bringing you closer to the Savior or further away? Are your feet guided by the Spirit or by your lusts? If you desire to be near the Savior, you must be led by the Spirit.

End Notes

[1]Walvoord, John. *The Holy Spirit.* Wheaton, Ill.: Van Kampen Press, 1954.

[2]Taylor, Dr. and Mrs. Howard. *Spiritual Secret of Hudson Taylor.* New Kensington, Penn.: Whitaker House, 1996. Pages 38-42. Used by permission of the publisher.

[3]Owen, John. *The Holy Spirit.* London: Banner of Truth, 1998. Pages 163-69. Used by permission.

Review Questions

1. What assurance does the new Christian have that he will be able to understand the Word of God?

2. For what general purpose does the Spirit empower a person?

3. Explain why a person must practice mortification daily.

4. How does the Spirit lead a person to truth?

5. Compare the two lists of fruits in Galatians 5:19-23. One list is a product of the flesh; one is a product of the Spirit. According to verses 13 through 24 which surround these lists, what is the key to having the fruit of the Spirit?

6. Read Romans 8 and state what the indwelling Spirit is seeking to do in the believer's life.

7. What sins are you seeking victory over in your life? Make a list of them and find what the Bible teaches about them. How will you gain victory over them?

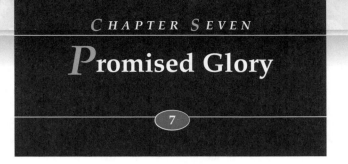

CHAPTER SEVEN

Promised Glory

7

The last works of the Spirit that we will look at concern both our present status and future hope. Through four different but related works, the Spirit promises us glory. The Spirit intercedes for this glory, seals us for this glory, is the down payment for this glory, and testifies to us that we are bound for this glory.

Although all of these works involve great theological truths, they also bring practical lessons for us. The Spirit's manifold ministries give believers great comfort and assurance regarding the future. Without these works, we would flounder without hope and confidence. By these works, we know that we shall see our Lord face to face.

The Spirit of Adoption

Being part of a family is a wonderful thing. There is comfort, refuge, joy, and "specialness." Every member belongs and has his or her role. It is a place of harmony and peace. I have great memories from childhood. Though my home was far from perfect, there was great comfort in knowing that I belonged. I was accepted because of the blood relationship. As a God-ordained institution, the family is supposed to model Christian love. It is also supposed to

A believer is placed into God's family both by birth and by adoption.

model other spiritual truths, particularly the Christian's relationship to God as a son to a father. A believer is placed into God's family both by birth and by adoption. We have already talked about the Spirit's work in the former (regeneration), and we will now talk about the latter aspect—biblical adoption.

In Romans 8:15, Paul states that we "have not received the spirit of bondage again to fear; but . . . the Spirit of adoption, whereby we cry, Abba, Father." One of the ministries of the Spirit to believers is His verification of adoption. Adoption is *the work of God that places a believer into full sonship.* It is a present blessing that we enjoy (Rom. 8:15). It is also a future event that we are awaiting, according to Romans 8:23: "And not only they, but ourselves also, which have the firstfruits of the Spirit, even we ourselves groan within ourselves, waiting for the adoption, to wit, the redemption of our body." That is different from how we normally think of adoption—the placing of a child unrelated by blood into a family. In the biblical context, a son who was adopted was already part of that family. At adoption, he received his full rights. He gained certain freedoms, financial blessings, and other rights.

	Physical	Spiritual
GET THE BIG PICTURE	Birth—member of the family	Regeneration—becomes a child of God
	Adoption—son receives full status	Adoption—believer receives the promised blessings of being a child of God

Similarly, at spiritual adoption, the believer receives all the promised blessings of being a child of God, some of which began at salvation, because he is already a child of God by regeneration. Although adoption will ultimately be fulfilled at a future time, we nevertheless have the Spirit of adoption within us now. He is called such because He assures us of certain truths pertaining to adoption.

"Well, you keep telling them to act like brothers and sisters."

1. **The Spirit of adoption assures us that we are indeed the children of God; we are sons bound for adoption.** "Ye have received the Spirit of adoption, whereby we cry, Abba, Father. The Spirit itself beareth witness with our spirit, that we are the children of God" (Rom. 8:15-16). The Spirit assures the believer that he has truly been born into the family of God. We have spiritual brothers and sisters in other believers. More importantly, we have a Father in heaven.

The word *Abba* is a highly personal and reverential name for God. It honors Him as *the Father.* It does not in any way diminish reverence for God; it actually does the reverse. It elevates Him as the Almighty Father whom we should respect and honor. But it also communicates the greatest possible relationship between us. God is our Father. Oh, the joy and wonder of this! We can go to our heavenly Father and ask Him to care and provide for us. The Bible is filled with truths concerning the Father's relationship to us. Our Father knows our needs (Matt. 6:8, 32), He knows how to give us good things (Matt. 7:11), He knows all the intricate details of our lives (Matt. 10:29-31), He gives peace (Rom. 1:7), and much more. In fact, our whole salvation was planned by the Father (Eph. 1:3-14), and He specifically predestined us to the adoption of sons (Eph. 1:5). We can conclude with the psalmist, "O that men would praise the Lord for his goodness, and for his wonderful works to the children of men!" (Ps. 107:8).

2. **The Spirit of adoption assures of bodily redemption.** Bodily redemption is one of the chief blessings of adoption. The Bible emphasizes that believers are eagerly "waiting for the adoption, to wit, the redemption of our body" (Rom. 8:23). In a sense, adoption will bring to completion the work of renewal when we receive glorified bodies. God will restore what was lost by Adam's Fall. According to I Corinthians 15:52, this change will happen "in a moment, in the twinkling of an eye." In many ways, we will be made like unto our elder brother—Christ. The blessings that the Father has poured out on His own Son will also be poured out on us. What is His shall be ours.

Regeneration is culminated in adoption.

3. **The Spirit of adoption confirms that we are no longer slaves.** Romans 8:15 emphasizes this truth, as does Galatians 4:4-7: "But when the fulness of the time was come, God sent forth his Son, made of a woman, made under the law, To redeem them that were under the law, that we might receive the adoption of sons. And because ye are sons, God hath sent forth the Spirit of his Son

into your hearts, crying, Abba, Father. Wherefore thou art no more a servant, but a son; and if a son, then an heir of God through Christ." There are many ramifications of this aspect of adoption, not the least of which is that we do not need to approach God in fear. Our bondage to sin has been broken. Our slavery to our former father, the Devil, has forevermore been broken. We are not slaves to sin, but sons of the Father. Understanding this truth will revolutionize your behavior and your service.

Although grasping both the present and future aspects of adoption can be difficult, we can rest assured that God has everything figured out. We can rely on Him who placed us as sons to finish His adoptive work. Having the Spirit of adoption within us should also compel us to purification. "Behold, what manner of love the Father hath bestowed upon us, that we should be called the sons of God. . . . Beloved, now are we the sons of God, and it doth not yet appear what we shall be: but we know that, when he shall appear, we shall be like him; for we shall see him as he is. And every man that hath this hope in him purifieth himself, even as he is pure" (I John 3:1-3). The joy of adoption is not a stagnant truth. It assures the believer of sonship, redemption, and broken bondage. It also compels him to greater purification. May the Holy Spirit himself give you great assurance of these truths if you have truly received Christ as your Savior.

The Spirit of Sealing

Ephesians 1:13 states, "In whom ye also trusted, after that ye heard the word of truth, the gospel of your salvation: in whom also after that ye believed, ye were sealed with that Holy Spirit of promise." Ephesians 4:30 states that we are sealed "unto the day of redemption." According to these verses and others, we are sealed with the Holy Spirit. But what exactly does it mean to be sealed by the Holy Spirit? In order to answer that question, we will have to travel back into history to gather information about seals.

What Is a Seal?

Throughout the history of the world, people have sent letters across towns, lands, and countries. It could be a letter from one businessman to another, from the apostle Paul to a church, from a king to a diplomat, or from a prince to a princess. If the document was very important or confidential, the sender needed a way to ensure that it would get to its destination safely. The sender might also have wanted a way to mark the genuineness and authenticity of his name. Forgers were common even back then. Out of these needs arose the invention of the seal, particularly the stamp seal for letters. The stamp seal consisted of two parts: the signet and the sealing substance. The signet (often a ring) was engraved with different markings. Depending on the time period in history, it could be the owner's name, a religious symbol, or name of the ruling king. A ruler's signet ring would have an intricate design so that it would not be reproducible. The sealing substance was often clay or another substance that would harden. When a person sealed something, he would roll the papyri tightly, affix a small amount of clay onto the edge of the letter, and press the signet into the clay, leaving its impression or seal. Only the sender or the receiver of the letter could break the seal. As mentioned before, the seal had a variety of uses: to designate ownership, to show authenticity, to impress a trademark, or to give authority to a document.

"You said the king wanted a seal that stands out, right?"

Who Seals?

Now that you know what a seal is, you need to know who seals us with the Spirit. In other words, if the Holy Spirit is the seal Himself, to whom does the signet impress belong? According to II Corinthians 1:21-22, it is God the Father: "Now he which stablisheth us with you in Christ, and hath anointed us, is God; who hath also sealed us, and given us the earnest of the Spirit in our hearts." This passage teaches that the Spirit within us is God the Father's seal. He has impressed His signet on our lives. These verses also teach that the sealing is universal for believers. Ephesians 1:13 says "In whom also after that ye believed, ye were sealed with that holy Spirit of promise." The Greek text could actually be translated, "Having also believed, you were sealed in Him with the Holy Spirit of promise" (NASB). Belief and sealing are simultaneous. When a person places his faith in the Son, the Father seals him with the Spirit.

Why Are Believers Sealed?

We can answer that question with three As: authority, authenticity, and assurance. First, the Spirit is our seal to show that we are under God's authority. He is our owner. Since He sealed us with His Spirit, He possesses our lives. All of our time belongs to Him. All of our skills and possessions are His. The seal of the Spirit, in effect, marks us as "His Majesty's Property." This is not a seal of bondage, though; it is a seal of freedom. We are free to serve Him, free to choose good, free to commune with God, and free to taste of heavenly delights. Being owned by God means that we are His precious treasures.

Second, the Spirit is our seal to show our authenticity. A Spirit-sealed person is a genuine believer. Romans 8:9 states that if you do not have the Spirit, you do not have Christ. This applies to sealing as well. The Spirit's seal identifies us as God's own. Just as an ancient seal testified to the earthly sender's identity, so also the Spirit testifies to the divine Sender's identity. The Spirit is God's divine stamp of genuineness. With this certainty, we can commend ourselves to the brethren as true believers (II Cor. 6:6).

Finally, and most importantly, the Spirit seals us to give assurance. Being sealed by the Spirit means that we are "tamper-proof." The seal of the Spirit gives the believer security in his salvation. We know that we are Christ's because of the Spirit (I John 4:13). According to Ephesians 4:30, we are sealed until the day of redemption. We can see how the Spirit's testimony of adoption and work of sealing merge together. The Spirit testifies of our coming adoption, the redemption of the body, to which the Spirit seals us. Our destiny is sealed for redemption. And only God the Father, the Sender and Receiver, can open His seal. That thought should provide all believers with great confidence and assurance in their lives. They should long for the coming of Christ when they shall be made like Him (I John 3:2).

This truth is an objective reality planned from eternity past. However, it is a truth that should not be abused. Being sealed does not give a person the license to sin. That is a perversion of truth. If a believer really understands His sealing, he should have a greater desire not to sin and disobey the Spirit: "And grieve not the holy Spirit of God, whereby ye are sealed unto the day of redemption" (Eph. 4:30). Sealing demands submission. The Spirit has sealed us with the holy and pure mark of God. And until we receive our sinless bodies in heaven, we must seek to live holy lives on earth. By the Spirit's power we can.

The Spirit of Earnest

The Holy Spirit is said to be our earnest or pledge. This is similar to the work of sealing. The word *earnest* is a synonym for pledge or down payment. There are three passages that teach this truth. Second Corinthians 1:22 states that God has "given the earnest of the Spirit in our hearts." Paul later adds in the same epistle, "Now he that hath wrought us for the selfsame thing is God, who also hath given unto us the earnest of the Spirit" (5:5). And in Ephesians 1:13-14, Paul writes, "Ye were sealed with that Holy Spirit of promise,

which is the earnest of our inheritance until the redemption of the purchased possession, unto the praise of his glory." All of these verses teach us that the Holy Spirit is our pledge of future glory. Just as you would give a down payment on a car, signifying a promise to make further payments, so also the Father gave us the Spirit as a down payment of future promises. He is our token pledge until that day.

That means we can be confident about God's promises. In II Corinthians 5:6-11, Paul follows his teaching about the earnest of the Spirit with these words:

> Therefore we are always confident, knowing that, whilst we are at home in the body, we are absent from the Lord: (For we walk by faith, not by sight:) We are confident, I say, and willing rather to be absent from the body, and to be present with the Lord. Wherefore we labour, that, whether present or absent, we may be accepted of him. For we must all appear before the judgment seat of Christ; that every one may receive the things done in his body, according to that he hath done, whether it be good

or bad. Knowing therefore the terror of the Lord, we persuade men; but we are made manifest unto God; and I trust also are made manifest in your consciences.

This passage teaches several applications of the Spirit's being our earnest. All of them have relevance for us today.

First, the earnest of the Spirit should instill confidence about the future (5:6-8). Being absent from the body means being present with the Lord. The down payment of the Spirit assures of this coming reality. Whether we enter the Lord's presence through death or through the Rapture, we can rest in this peace-giving truth. The Spirit of adoption testifies that we shall some day be fully redeemed, the Spirit of sealing guarantees that we will reach that day of redemption, and the Spirit of earnest is a present down payment of that day of redemption. Just as the indwelling Spirit assures of communion with God now, the earnest of the Spirit assures us of communion with God then. Truly our salvation is a marvelous masterpiece that could only be designed by an omniscient God.

The Spirit of earnest is a present down payment of that day of redemption.

Next, the earnest of the Spirit necessitates labor now (5:9-10). Knowing that we will someday enter the Lord's presence, we should be eager to serve today. Paul extends the imagery of the earnest of the Spirit to include the investment idea: we should be laboring to yield great returns on His investment. Ephesians 1:14 adds that this investment return is ultimately the praise of God's glory. God receives great glory when saints reach their day of redemption. What a joy it is, therefore, to labor now to bring returns on the Lord's investment. Some will bring thirty-fold back, some sixty-fold, and some one hundred-fold (Mark 4:20). May the Spirit's pledge increase our productivity for the Lord.

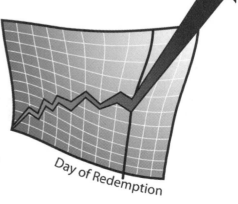

Day of Redemption

Lastly, the Spirit's pledge should encourage us to witness (II Cor. 5:11). We should want all men to enjoy the privileges and blessings that await us. How selfish it is for a Christian to be unfaithful with his stewardship of grace! Knowing that God was gracious enough to invest His Spirit in you should make you gracious enough to invest yourself in others. God intended that His Spirit indwell us permanently as a seal and an earnest so that we would have power to give the gospel. By submitting to the Spirit's leading, we are empowered to persuade men. Just as Paul claimed the Spirit's power to witness in Romans 15:19 and I Corinthians 2:4, we also must claim it. Let us labor to see the salvation of our fellow men.

The Spirit of Intercession

The final work of the Spirit that we will study is His work of intercession. In Zechariah 12:10, God promised that He would pour out "the Spirit of grace and of supplications." This explains why the Spirit is often called the Spirit of prayer. He searches and knows what is the mind of the Father and prays for His divine will to be accomplished. This work is further expounded in Romans 8:26-27. "Likewise the Spirit also helpeth our infirmities: for we know not what we should pray for as we ought: but the Spirit itself maketh intercession for us with groanings which cannot be uttered. And he that searcheth the hearts knoweth what is the mind of the Spirit, because he maketh intercession for the saints according to the will of God." The Spirit's work of intercession is a comforting and hope-giving reality of the Christian faith. We are so weak that we often do not even know what to pray for. We see our circumstances and predicaments, and our limited minds do not know how to pray for them. Oh, we may pray what we think is best, but it is the Spirit who takes these prayers and strengthens them before the throne of God. He gives help to our weaknesses.

But not only that, He also makes personal intercession for us. He asks the Father to meet spiritual, physical, and emotional needs that we do not even know we have. The groanings by which He gives His prayers cannot be uttered. That does not mean that His prayers are in encrypted languages. Rather, it means that they are beyond our comprehension and understanding. Give praise to the Spirit that He intercedes on our behalf.

Spirit's Intercession

Believer's Prayer

His intercessions are always heard and answered. Whereas we may not pray according to the Lord's will, the Spirit always intercedes according to the will of God. We can be sure then that His prayers are heard. What hope should spring in your heart that God the Spirit intercedes for you and that His prayers are always answered! It is through the Spirit that we abound in hope: "Now the God of hope fill you with all joy and peace in believing, that ye may abound in hope, through the power of the Holy Ghost" (Rom. 15:13).

What specifically does the Spirit pray for? Though no answer could include all the possibilities, it seems likely within the context of Romans 8 that the Spirit intercedes for the completion of our salvation and for our conformity to the Savior, which brings together all four of the works discussed in this chapter. The Spirit of adoption testifies to future redemption, seals us for that redemption, is the down payment for that redemption, and intercedes for our future redemption. The confidence a believer gains from studying these truths is overwhelming.

Our own prayers should be guided by the Spirit and subject to His will. That is what "praying in the Holy Ghost" means (Jude 20). It is allowing Him to guide your prayers in their content. It also means that the Spirit is empowering you to pray as you should. It is only through the Spirit that we have an entrance to God's throne (Eph. 2:18). Therefore, we should be praying in the Spirit at all times (Eph. 6:18). The harmony of the Spirit's and believers' prayers should be characteristic of the church. They should be one voice as in Revelation 22:17: "And the Spirit and the bride say, Come." May we all respond as the apostle John did in verse 20: "Amen. Even so, come, Lord Jesus."

Conclusion

The following hymn brings together all the major works of the Spirit that you have studied. As you read the words to this hymn, concentrate on the different works of the Spirit, and may the words reflect the sincere prayer of your heart.

To Thee, the Great Eternal Dove

To Thee, the great eternal Dove,
  the God of life, and truth, and love,

With hearts unchained Thy praise we sing,
  with tongues unloosed our tribute bring.

For Thou art holy, gracious, true;
  For Thou, Jehovah, made us new.

With life and hope Thou set us free
  and gave us light and liberty.

Indwelling Spirit, make us know
  our Lord and Savior here below.

Unveil His face that we may see
  our Head and Prince, our Sovereignty.

Unmold our hearts from sin and shame,
  a temple fit for His pure Name.

Unite our hearts in singleness,
  a body joined in Christlikeness.

O Holy Pledge, our Great Earnest,
  who guarantees our endless rest,

Assure us still of future bliss,
  redemption's hope of sinlessness.

O blessed Seal, our Surety,
  who fixed secure eternity,

We beg Thy prayers to intercede,
  with groanings strong for us to plead.

Almighty Dove and gracious Guide,
  control our lives, o'er us preside

That we may know Thy leading light
  and use Thy gifts in holy might.

Submitted now we ask for grace;
  with faith and pow'r our hearts embrace.

Almighty God, our lives transform,
  to Christ's own likeness us conform.

Review Questions

1. Why is the sealing of the believer necessary?

2. In light of our discussion on the Spirit of adoption, what are some appropriate responses? How should this truth change your behavior?

3. The Spirit's prayers are always answered. Why aren't believers' prayers always answered?

4. Explain why we have the Spirit as an earnest.

5. Do you think Christians should pray for the Spirit's intercession?

6. Explain the differences between a slave and a son in the biblical context.

7. Make a list of the works of the Spirit that you have learned. Which ones have had the greatest influence on you and why?

How Then Shall We Walk?

Do you remember those hard questions that I asked you in the introduction to the book?

Does Scripture support the deity of the Holy Spirit? If so, how?

What specific activities does the Holy Spirit perform in the salvation of a sinner?

What is the believer's relationship to the Holy Spirit?

How should a Christian evaluate modern claims regarding tongues and Spirit baptism?

Hopefully, they aren't as hard any more. Having looked at almost all the references to the Spirit in the Bible, you should be able to give much better answers. You also probably realize that there is so much more than what is covered in those four general questions. They represent just a skimming of the many wonderful truths concerning the Spirit. Now I have a harder question for you.

Has your life changed since you have gained a better understanding of the Spirit's work? Is there any fruit that He has produced? Any change in your life? I hope that by God's grace you understand how vital your response to the Spirit is. Head change is not enough; the heart must change as well. If you truly want to see the Spirit work in your life, you must submit to Him.

Friend, if you have come to realize that you are not regenerated, that you have never believed in Christ as your Savior, won't you do so now? The Spirit's convicting you of sin, righteousness, and judgment will not continue indefinitely. Although the Spirit is longsuffering, you do not know how long He will endure your insulting His grace. Repent and believe now, and Christ will pour out His Spirit on you. O the fountain of life that awaits you if you will but believe! The Spirit longs to give you life, hope, peace, and assurance. What hinders you from taking this offer of grace?

Without the Spirit, you will remain in darkness and sin. With the Spirit, you will walk in light and have joy everlasting.

Believer, if you have realized how calloused your heart has grown, how unsubmissive you have become, won't you repent and return? The Father will forgive you and restore unto you the joy of your salvation. You will not have rest until you yield to the Spirit. Stop grieving Him and trying to quench His work in your life. Submit to the Lord now, and He will lead you by His Holy Word.

My heart's desire is that you will draw closer to Christ by applying the truths of Scripture and that your changed belief will lead to changed behavior. I trust that during this study you have allowed the Spirit to purge and refine you so that you are free to walk according to truth. For "where the Spirit of the Lord is, there is liberty" (II Cor. 3:17).

> "Now unto him that is able to keep you from falling, and to present you faultless before the presence of his glory with exceeding joy, To the only wise God our Saviour, be glory and majesty, dominion and power, both now and ever. Amen" (Jude 24-25).